THE DRINKING WOMAN

Revisited

THE DRINKING WOMAN

Revisited

EDITH LYNN HORNIK-BEER

All rights reserved, including without limitation the right to reproduce this book or any portion thereof in any form or by any means, whether electronic or mechanical, now known or hereinafter invented, without the express written permission of the publisher.

First edition published by Association Press

Copyright © 1977 by Edith Lynn Hornik-Beer

Cover art by Mayling E. Simpson
Cover design by Olivia Brodtman

ISBN: 978-1-5040-4063-1

Distributed in 2017 by Open Road Distribution
180 Maiden Lane
New York, NY 10038
www.openroadmedia.com

CONTENTS

Foreword by the late FRANK A. SEIXAS, M.D.,
former Medical Director of National Council on Alcoholism vii
Acknowledgments ix
Introduction by Thomas P. Beresford, M.D. xiii
A Few Words From the Author xvii

1. A Woman an Alcoholic-Never! 3
2. Alcohol and Alcoholism Defined 10
3. You're Just Like Your Parents-Maybe? 26
4. Pregnancy 31
5. Stress and Family Living 37
6. The Alcoholic Woman in the Unhealthy Marriage 52
7. Female Sexuality and Alcoholism 63
8. Feminism 82
9. The Cultural Stress Factor: I 97
10. The Cultural Stress Factor: II 114
11. Life With an Alcoholic 127
12. Alcoholics Anonymous 141
13. Seeking Help 149
14. Getting Ready to Face the World Again 176

Epilogue: Rebuilding 185
Notes and Readings 187

FOREWORD

Edith Lynn Hornik has done it again! As a sequel to her popular book, You and Your Alcoholic Parent, she has taken up the theme of The Drinking Woman, and, with painstaking research (documented by bibliographies at the end of the chapters), much travel to facilities where women are receiving treatment for alcoholism, interviews with a large number of the women themselves, the people who are caring for such women, and those performing research studies, she has come up with a volume that strongly retains her own individuality which will engage many, instruct many, and give hope to many.

Historical references which go back to the Greeks and Persians, a tart evaluation of Carrie Nation, and wide-ranging attention to Eskimos, the Irish, and Indians are informed by many simple illustrative case histories.

We need attention to the problem of women and alcoholism. The National Council on alcoholism has developed a task force to address this problem. The National Institute of Alcohol Abuse and Alcoholism is giving special emphasis to it. The Women's Liberation Movement has encouraged bringing female alcoholism out of the closet.

FOREWORD

Women have been neglected also in alcoholism research, and new studies are finding physiological differences in their reactions to alcohol, which are of importance. The rhythms of their lives, their goals, and their interaction with society, spouse, and child are all perforce different from those of men—and not less important. They can no longer be sloughed off.

This book will be welcomed by many who need the help it offers, the encouragement to seek treatment, and the knowledge of where that help may be obtained. Besides, she has made it interesting. Interest in and knowledge of alcoholism are advancing. So far, the massive number of people suffering is still far more than the means to stem the disease. But we see glimpses in the individuals who recover, and in the increasing numbers who have recovered, that the hope sprinkled liberally through this book for individuals will some day be summated into the turning of the tide for the disease. So, while the search continues for a "short cut"—a technological shortcut to social change—the application of the silent case finding of a woman reading a book alone and the ability to find the treatment proposed by this book will do much good.

FRANK A. SEIXAS, M.D., 1977
Medical Director
National Council on Alcoholism

ACKNOWLEDGMENTS

This book could not have been written without the encouragement, enthusiasm and cooperation of many doctors, social workers, directors of treatment centers, and recovered women alcoholics who now work professionally in the field of alcoholism. My special thanks go to Albert M. Browne-Mayers, M.D., associate medical director of the National Council on Alcoholism for his selfless advice and help on all facets of this subject.

My thanks also go to:
Frank Seixas, M.D., medical director, National Council on Alcoholism, New York
Mark Keller, editor, Journal of Alcohol Studies, New Brunswick, New Jersey
Timothy G. Coffey, managing editor, Journal of Alcohol Studies, New Brunswick, NJ
Rabbi Sheldon Zimmerman, Central Synagogue, New York, N.Y.
Jan Du Plain, program director on women, National Council on Alcoholism
Emily Bergson, M.S.W., Appleton House, McLean Hospital, Belmont, Massachusetts

ACKNOWLEDGMENTS

Margaret Rudolph, executive director, Association of Halfway Houses, Alcoholism Programs of North America Inc., St. Paul, Minnesota

Sharon C. Wilsnack, Ph.D., director, Regional Alcoholism Rehabilitation Program, Bloomington, Indiana

Clara B. Synigal, director, Interim House, Philadelphia, Pennsylvania

Ben Morgan Jones, Ph.D., associate director, Oklahoma Center for Alcohol and Drug Related Studies, Oklahoma City, Oklahoma

Marilyn K. Jones, M.A.T., supervisor, Laboratory of Women Studies, University of Oklahoma, Oklahoma City, Oklahoma

Charles E. Becker, M.D., chairman of pharmacology, San Francisco Medical Center, San Francisco, California.

Charles S. Poole, M.D., Ob/Gyn., attending obstetrician and gynecologist, White Plains Hospital Medical Center, White Plains, New York

Stanley Gitlow, M.D., clinical professor of Medicine, Mt, Sinai School of Medicine, New York.

Fred T. Davis, M.S.W., deceased

Henry B. Murphree, M.D., C.M., professor of psychiatry and pharmacology, Rutgers Medical School, New Brunswick, N.J.

Henry Rosett, M.D., associate professor of psychiatry, Boston University School of Medicine, Boston, Massachusetts

Wanda Frog, director, North American Indian Women's Council on Chemical Dependencies, Spooner, Wisconsin

Donald Goodwin, M.D., professor of psychiatry, chairman of the department, University of Kansas Medical Center, College of Health Sciences and Hospital, Kansas City, Kansas George Winokur, M.D., professor and chairman of psychiatry, University of Iowa Medical School, Iowa City, Iowa

Eva Rado, M.D., assistant professor of psychiatry, New York Medical College, Valhalla, New York

Kenneth Williams, M.D., assistant professor of psychiatry and internal medicine, University of Pittsburgh School of Medicine, Pittsburgh, Pennsylvania

Erma Polly Williams, M.R.E., Rutgers Center of Alcohol Studies, New Brunswick, New Jersey

* * *

ACKNOWLEDGMENTS

All the Al-Anon and Alcoholics Anonymous groups who not only welcomed me but gave me access to their case histories, and who in some instances invited groups of women alcoholics into their private homes so that we could talk intimately. Most of the case histories in this book came from meetings with these open-hearted women.

My editor, Mr. Robert Roy Wright, who was always ready to listen to my "thinking out loud," and, finally, to my family, Joe, Robby and Abigail, who took such good care of themselves whenever I traveled out of town to research this book. I am grateful to Jane Armstrong, the librarian at Rutgers Center of Alcohol Studies, who always informed me about the latest studies available, and who seems to smile through all confusion and adversity, and to Betty Gold, librarian at National Council on Alcoholism who saved all new publications for me.

Working on this book has been for me a deeply moving experience. As I researched and wrote and revised, I realized that many of the problems, faced by alcoholic women have a relationship to the problems faced by all women. I hope I have given as much of myself in work, spirit and knowledge as I learned from all the admirable women I met.

We are presently in the year 2016, thirty-nine years since The Drinking Woman was first published. Much has changed. We now have the internet where we can buy books on line and where I have noticed that old copies of The Drinking Woman are selling at inflated prices. I reread the book and learned that not much has changed for The Drinking Woman . Women still have to deal with prejudices, stress, and inherited susceptibility to addiction. The studies on Fetal Alcohol Syndrome, family dynamics, alcohol and its interplay with the menstrual cycle, just to mention a few studies, have not changed. Thanks to Authors Guild, I am republishing The Drinking Woman. At the end of each chapter I have added the latest studies, medical updates, therapy innovations and the most recent statistics on alcoholism in the hope that it will aid today's reader.

Edith Lynn Hornik-Beer

More Acknowledgements

My thanks go to those who have helped me update *The Drinking Woman*. They have given their time to point out the vital works and

ACKNOWLEDGMENTS

studies that make a difference in our understanding of this disease, alcoholism, and how it effects in particular women be they young, teenagers, middle age or elderly. I would like to acknowledge two librarians who aided my research by procuring medical books from out of area libraries.

My thanks go to:

Kevin Williams Colorado Mountain College Steamboat Springs Library, Colorado; Michelle Dover Circulation Services Manager at Bud Werner Memorial Library, Steamboat Springs, Colorado

A major thank you goes to Dr. Thomas P. Beresford who not only guided me to the latest research but also proofed my updates. Dr. Beresford is an internationally known physician and medical scientist in alcohol and drug use disorders. He is best known for his research work in alcoholism and liver transplant, aging and alcoholism, and the brain disorders of alcoholism.

Dr. Beresford holds appointments as Physician with the Department of Veterans Affairs and as Professor of Psychiatry at the School of Medicine of the University of Colorado. He is part of the Editorial Board of National Council on Alcoholism and Drug Dependence (NCADD) Medical-Scientific Committee. Above all Dr. Beresford is a compassionate and understanding physician.

INTRODUCTION
BY THOMAS P. BERESFORD, MD

Alcoholism is a complex phenomenon that may best be thought of as due to an interaction of environmental and genetic factors. The lion's share of them occur in the heritage of cultural and social mores rather than in the realm of DNA. Vaillant, in *The Natural History Of Alcoholism, Revisited*, for example, presents no less than eight different factors that appear to be etiologically related to alcohol addiction. Only one of them—an innate insensitivity to the effects of alcohol—can be said to reflect the biological variations directly attributable to gene effects. And that appears to be a complex effect involving many genes. A Mendelian genetic model does not apply: there is no Dominant Homozygous condition that turns people into alcoholics.

It is true, however, that in order to become an alcoholic, one must drink beverages that contain alcohol. It is this to which Edith Lynn Hornik turned her, and our, attention over 30 years ago in her first edition of *The Drinking Woman*. When that book first came out, the Women's Movement—that vast cultural change in US society and in most "developed" nations in the world—was hardly more than a few years old. With the passage of time, Edith revisits what was then the

INTRODUCTION BY THOMAS P. BERESFORD, MD

new ground of sociological change in respect to women and alcohol use. At that time, for example, few in this nation had ever heard of the fetal alcohol syndrome, a condition first described during the Gin Epidemic of 18th-century England. Now, some states in the US have warning labels on alcoholic beverages advising against alcohol use during pregnancy.

Conversely, the fact that women who drink heavily have a higher relative frequency than men of the most serious forms of alcoholic liver disease, namely alcoholic cirrhosis, was known far longer than 40 years ago. Molecular science has yet to tell us why this is. Socially, however, the traditional "protection" thought to be conferred by female gender in respect to developing alcoholism—a four-to-one male-dominated illness—appears to be waning as more women drink alcohol and find they lose the ability to control their alcohol use, leading to heavy, and dangerous, drinking. The essence of alcoholism—the loss of control of alcohol use such that one cannot predict with consistent reliability how much alcohol one will consume from one episode to the next—does not appear to respect to gender differences. At least, it does not do so in and of the single absence or presence of the Y chromosome.

Some argue that women may be more vulnerable to developing alcoholism because of a dose effect of alcohol in the smaller average physical volumes of women as compared to men. Many question this assertion, however, and find it more likely that other variables—such as the availability of alcohol, its cost, and the social mores that make it more attractive to women—are more to the point. It is these on which Edith Hornik focuses in *The Drinking Woman*, not only in understanding the differential causes of alcoholism for women. She looks further to understanding its effects, preventing its occurrence, treating it when it occurs, and, most importantly, the necessary ingredients for preventing relapses in this chronic condition.

Thirty plus years after its first publication, *The Drinking Woman* continues to ask salient questions where sufficient answers have not been found. As Ms. Hornik intended in the first edition, however, it remains a very hopeful and optimistic examination of female alcoholism. Whether in women, or in men, alcoholism is a treatable illness from the point of view of the scientific model. And it is this hope for improvement and recovery that her volume provides. Where in some instances alcoholism can be especially devastating in women, it remains an illness of hope in working through the unresolved ambivalence toward uncontrolled drinking and on toward physical health and a return to personal growth.

A FEW WORDS FROM THE AUTHOR

"It's about time someone wrote a book about where it's at for the alcoholic woman." That's what a woman murmured as she was being discharged from a drying-out facility. She was talking about what the drinking experience does to a woman's life and to a woman's body, how it differs from a man's physical experience. A woman's general reaction to alcohol is affected by her menstrual cycles, menopause and the extra fatty tissues nature gives women. If pregnant, be it married or as a single mom, the alcohol she ingests, even if it is just a few drinks to relax, may impair the child she is carrying.

Sexually a drinking woman is as well vulnerable. The drinking man may perform poorly. He might not even remember the next day with whom he tried to have intercourse and laugh it off as a fun night. The drinking woman might perform poorly sexually, not remember with whom she tried to have intercourse, and find herself with an unwanted pregnancy. Try and laugh that one off.

Even though we hope that society's tolerance of a drinking woman is today no different than our understanding of an alcoholic man there exists still a fine distinction. A woman is considered the mother of us all. Mother may be sophisticated, go to bars and drink, but she can't get drunk, or drink "like a man." Many women are still afraid to come forth and say, "I have a drinking problem." They are afraid, because "I might lose my job," "What will the neighbors say?" "Will they take my children away?" and if she is elderly, "Will my children take away my power of attorney?" Those who are married are afraid of what their husbands will say. Statistics have shown that a husband will divorce his alcoholic wife more readily than a wife her alcoholic husband. If she is a single mother she is afraid that if she goes into treatment she won't be able to support her children. If she is a teenager she will try to keep it from her parents who might take her driving privileges away. However, these women suffer as much as any man. The alcoholism patterns, the camouflaging of hangovers, the denials of drinking, the hiding of bottles from the family, and rationalizing the drinking are common to most alcoholics, whether man or woman. Later on, as the disease progresses, a woman dependent on alcohol is as susceptible to D.T.'s (Delirium Tremens) as a man. She suffers tremors, untold discomfort, and the unpleasant withdrawal symptoms that drive all too many back to drink.

These are women who have a disease known as alcoholism. Whether they are secret drinkers or the loud ones in public places, their distasteful action is a byproduct of a disease as serious and as real as cancer, heart disease, or diabetes.

Women of all walks of life can be alcoholics. The woman who has a job, who stays at home to take care of her family (many women while actively drinking maintain a neat house), the woman with a college degree, her own money, the woman who lives in the ghetto, in a mansion, the woman who married the president of the bank, or the chief of police, or the local tailor, the woman who is active in the church, in the synagogue, who is in your local car pool, is as susceptible as anyone else to being, or becoming an alcoholic.

Alcoholism often takes its toll during middle age. For a woman, her menopause ("The children don't need me anymore," "My husband finds the women at work better looking than he does me," "I am nothing but another lonely widow. What is there to get up for this morning?") or the loss of a career ("I lost my job," "Job interviews are the pits," "They only want young women") can encourage her to turn to the bottle.

A FEW WORDS FROM THE AUTHOR

There are many other factors: the need to medicate an undiagnosed mental illness, a hereditary component, an unhappy youth, sexual abuse, a frustrated career, an unwanted divorce, an inferior view of oneself. All may contribute to excessive drinking.

The Drinking Woman Revisited helps the reader to come to terms with what life is like for the alcoholic woman, what her family can do to help her, what independent attitudes may help her to see her way clear to a new and better life, where she can go for help and understanding, and finally, how can she pick up the pieces when her family has abandoned her.

Edith Lynn Hornik-Beer

THE DRINKING WOMAN

Revisited

CHAPTER 1

A WOMAN AN ALCOHOLIC—NEVER!

Women need to have alcoholism defined in terms that include them. For all too many years, researchers have ignored the female alcoholic or simply assumed that the "few women" who are alcoholics suffer no differently than the men. Only lately have we begun to recognize the importance of looking at women separately from men. Even how a woman drinks is different from the way a man drinks. Women tend to mix prescribed medicine with alcohol more than do men. Women also tend to pursue a pattern of continual drinking, while men tend towards bouts of drinking.

In many works on alcoholism to which we still refer today, women aren't even mentioned, and then only as those who have to live with alcoholic husbands, seldom as the one who may be the drinker. In *A Dictionary of Words About Alcohol*, a standard and much-used reference book, which came out in 1968 and has not been updated, Keller and McCormick, when dealing with some of the more important definitions, quote verbatim from studies done on men only. In no part of the dictionary are there definitions quoting specifically the female experience with alcohol. For example, under the words compensating drinker, the dictionary cites the type of man who uses alcohol to cope with deep feelings of inferiority, especially if he is gifted. Or, the dictionary refers to the decadent drinker as a man who drinks to deal with boredom. Is one to assume that a woman never seeks alcohol to relieve her boredom or feeling of inferiority? It's painful enough being an alcoholic. But a woman must feel doubly bad, because—if these definitions are to be accepted—she is intruding on a man's disease.

As recently as 1972, Dr. Marc Shuckit, a psychiatrist specializing in the field of alcoholism, noted that between 1929 and 1970 there were only 29 studies on women alcoholics published in the English language.

One can only guess why women were omitted from the majority of studies. Perhaps few women could be found among the tested populations. This would be the case in the Veterans Administration hospitals, for example, which until very recently were populated by men only. But studies and dictionaries and populations in hospitals alone cannot be the entire reason for women alcoholics not being noted. We shall need to search deeper if we are to find the real reasons for this neglect.

Most basic, perhaps, is the fact that society hates to see a woman off her pedestal. It is easier for society to talk about mastectomy than about female alcoholism. The history of women has made it difficult for society to understand that a woman can be predisposed to alcoholism. Our understanding of women and alcohol remains a vestige of the days of the Woman's Christian Temperance Union and of Carrie Nation.

Carrie Nation and the WCTU

Carrie Nation, a very tall woman of unusual strength, smashed up saloons with her hatchet. She called it "hatchetations of joints." She was arrested about thirty times for her "hatchetations." She lectured, spoke at carnivals and sold souvenir hatchets, making enough money to pay her fines and to build a home for the wives of alcoholics in Kansas City. This energetic woman wrote a meandering autobiography in 1904, *The Use and Need of the Life of Carrie A. Nation*. Carrie Nation's first husband was an alcoholic and the marriage was, needless to say, unhappy. Her second husband was a lawyer and minister, and it was during this marriage that she began her embittered campaign against alcohol. She was also against corsets and such things as short skirts. She was given to mystic seizures and appears to have suffered from hereditary paranoia. Her mother was a psychotic who believed herself to be Queen Victoria.

The suffragettes and the Woman's Christian Temperance Union looked upon Carrie Nation as an unbalanced person, and she received small support from them. Nevertheless, Carrie Nation left a lasting, crippling image of a non-drinking woman who worked for prohibition.

The WCTU started in 1873 as a temperance group crusade. As the organization grew, it adopted a wide ranging platform which included home protection, the following of the golden rule, and labor and prison reform. These women faced squarely the social problems of their day. They pointed out political corruption, advocated kindergartens, and wanted to initiate badly needed social and family services. They asked for women's right to vote and prohibition of liquor traffic. Without labeling liquor abuse as a medical problem, the WCTU made the world aware of the problem of drinking.

Indeed, so strongly did the women advocate prohibition at the same time they were advocating their right to vote that the following message came across: "Give us the right to vote, and we the women will protect you from alcohol."

This was an attitude men could understand. It was in line with their image of women. These ladies were so overbearing that no one ever thought that any women, except those who hung around bars, or were "loose," could possibly have a drinking problem.

Ancient History, Alcohol and Women

Of course, this attitude, "ladies don't drink," is unrealistic. Women and alcohol are entwined throughout our recorded history. In some ancient cultures, women had an active part in the drinking ceremonies and in the drinking folklore. In Greece, Bacchus, the wine god, was the most popular. His female devotees, the Maenads, worshipped him in drunken frenzies. Clay tablets unearthed from the ruins of ancient Babylon reveal the Babylonians to have been familiar with beer in 5000 B.C. The brewers, all women, were priestesses who brewed the beer in their holy temples. The Egyptians considered the knowledge of how to brew beer as a gift imparted to them by their goddess of nature, Isis.

There is a revealing Persian legend about King Jamshid, who ruled Persia several thousand years before the birth of Christ. The king was fond of grapes, and after a particular fruitful harvest, he ordered the surplus grapes stored in jars. When he was ready to eat them, he found that the grapes had burst and fermented. Not knowing what this strange liquid was, he ordered it stored and labeled "poison." One of the ladies of the court who felt lonely and depressed decided to end it all with the King's "poison." After a few swallows of the "poison," she felt happier, and after a few more swallows, fell into a comfortable sleep. The next morning she told the king his "poison" was not a poison at all but an elixir. If she continued to seek solace in that cellar, this legendary lady from King Jamshid's court may just have become the first woman alcoholic.

As long as women have known about alcohol, they have experienced the pressures and problems of alcoholism. Aristotle talked about, "foolish, drunken or hare-brain women." The popular author of *Tom Jones*, Henry Fielding, mentioned in 1751, in one of his many pamphlets, women problem drinkers, ". . . an infant who is conceived in Gin? With the poisonous distillations of which it is nourished, both in the womb and at the breast." A few years later, Charles Dickens alluded to female drinking in his *Pickwick Papers*.

It was not unusual, before the age of anesthetics, for doctors to prescribe an opiate to a woman who was in pain during childbirth. It is said that two-thirds of the opiate users in the 19th century were women. Other doctors advocated alcohol to alleviate discomfort during pregnancy and delivery, as well as a relaxant in premenstrual tension, and for preventing infection after childbirth. Beer was thought to fortify a woman for breast feeding. Over the counter, women could buy Lydia Pinkham's tonic or Peruna, which had a high content of alcohol. So did grandma's special blueberry tonic.

A woman who was an alcoholic was not called "neurotic" as in our tranquilized society, but was called "hysterical," or almost any name but alcoholic. Women alcoholics themselves preferred these terms because they were confused by their need for liquor. They found it inconsistent with their role as mother, wife, or well-mannered spinster.

Even today a woman finds it difficult to accept the thought that she may be an alcoholic. We still wish to perceive a woman as the one who is good, who would show her discomfort only by being ill-tempered, difficult, or sickly. Never, never as an alcoholic.

Alcoholism and Women Today

According to the National Council on Alcoholism, there are approximately 10 million alcoholics in the USA. It is difficult to estimate how many of these are women. Some help agencies claim that women alcoholics outnumber men alcoholics. The social workers and visiting nurses who observe the lonely female senior citizen who has outlived her husband, as most women do, come into daily contact with more women than men who take up drinking in desperation. Alcoholics Anonymous, a prominent self-help group, notes that while one out of four of their present members are women, women account for one out of three of their "new" members. AA does not know whether this increase is indicative of an increase in female alcoholics or whether it means only that women today are less afraid to seek help.

Whether the alcoholic be a man or a woman, young or old, the family may well not want to recognize a drinking, problem in its midst. It is especially easy to shield a woman or a girl for "the sake of her own good name and reputation." The mother of a school-age daughter may simply ignore the warning signals the school or the law enforcement officials may point out to her, and say to them, "Thank heaven she's not on grass." She may tell her daughter to "watch your reputation among the boys." If a woman is a widow or divorced, her sons and daughters, especially if they are of the middle and upper class, may find it easiest "as long as Mom is leading her own life" to ignore the situation. If she is a married woman, policemen have been known to have arrangements with husbands to phone them when their wives were picked up.

Such protected women may be sent to private doctors who may tell them to cut down on their drinking. Or they may be sent to a private clinic for a vitamin cure. If wealthy enough, the woman alcoholic may be put under the care of a private nurse or simply left to her own devices. The family of one such alcoholic woman put her in an apartment in a completely different part of town, paid her rent and gave her grocery money which, of course, kept her in liquor. Lady that she was, she didn't even go out for her bottles. The best store in town delivered them.

The saddest part of such an attitude is the fact that the family of the alcoholic may never know that alcoholism is a disease, that it is an arrestable disease, and that as long as the alcoholic drinks actively it is affecting the whole family. It is unrealistic to act as if women never drank. Women need information about alcohol and alcoholism as much as men. The time has come to stop ostracizing the female alcoholic. We need to stop saying, "A woman alcoholic—Never!" and instead say, "Yes, there are women alcoholics. Let's help her. Let's look the problem squarely in the face."

UPDATES:
- In 1994 the National Institute of Health published guidelines concerning the inclusion of women and minorities as subjects in clinical research. Consequently researchers consider carefully today the psychosocial and biological gender differences and how these facts need to influence treatment.
- SAMHSA (Substance Abuse and Mental Health Services Administration) in 2006 pointed out that approximately 40% of substance abuse treatment facilities now provide special programs for women. This may include therapy geared to women and overnight facilities for children while their mothers are in treatment.
- According to Alcoholic Anonymous' estimates women in 1968 counted as 22% of AA membership. Presently women make up about 35% of AA membership. It is not known whether these numbers mean that women are more willing to reach out for help or that more women are drinking.
- Alcohol abuse was three times as high in men as compared to women according to the National Epidemiologic Survey on Alcohol and Related Conditions (NESARC) in 2004. College women may now drink as much as their fellow male

students. CASA (the National Center on Addiction and Substance Abuse at Columbia University), a nonprofit drug abuse research group, reported a 16% rise between 1993 and 2005 in the number of full-time college students who acknowledge frequent binge drinking. But binge drinking was up 22% in women, nearly double the increase in men. At the same time, 37% of college women said they drank on 10 or more occasions in the last month.

- Prescription drugs and over-the-counter pain reliever abuse in women continues to be high. (SAMHSA 2006)
- Dr. George E. Valliant, psychiatrist and Professor at Harvard Medical School and Director of Research for the Department of Psychiatry, indicated that according to a study by Robins and Smith in 1980 our understanding of alcoholism in women is still extremely sketchy. He says, "For example, in the United Kingdom the male-to-female ratio of arrests for drunkenness is 14:1; for psychiatric hospitalizations for alcoholism it is 5:1; and yet for cirrhosis, the male-to-female ratio is 1:1. How are we to interpret such data?"

CHAPTER 2

ALCOHOL AND ALCOHOLISM DEFINED

Alcohol is a drug, and to the best of our knowledge, the first manmade drug. The alcohol we drink, ethyl alcohol, is produced naturally by the process of fermentation. A microscopic plant called yeast floats freely in the air and reacts with the sugar in the juice. This reaction produces alcohol and releases carbon dioxide in the air. When about 14% of the juice is alcohol, it stops the process of the yeast. The liquid left is wine or beer.

Since alcohol can be produced naturally in any sugar-containing mixture such as fruit, honey or grains, historians feel that alcohol was discovered accidentally in prehistoric times.

In the Middle Ages, an alchemist named Gerber searched for a means to turn dirt into gold. He heated wine or beer in a still to 173° F. The alcohol boiled off as a vapor, but the water and most of the other ingredients in the liquid remained in the still. Then he cooled the vapor, obtaining almost pure alcohol.

Although Gerber wrote about his discovery only as a scientific experiment, some 500 years later Arnauld de Villeneuve, a 13th-century professor of medicine at the University of Montpellier in France, rediscovered alcohol. He called it aqua vitae, the "water of life." He said,

"This name is remarkably suitable since it is really a water of immortality. It prolongs life, clears away ill humors, revives the heart and maintains youth."

As was discussed earlier, alcohol was used to help women when in pain. It was also used by men and children. Brandy was given for treating faintness, wine for blood-building, and alcoholic beverages in general for sleeplessness, over-excitement, to stimulate a poor appetite.

Whiskey was the only known antidote for snake bites. And many a man today still claims it is as effective as any serum.

Sometimes alcohol is effective. Wine is still recommended today to elderly people to cheer them and to block out vague aches and pains. Some nursing homes serve wine with their meals. Wine is mentioned in the Old Testament and is still used by men and women in both Jewish and Christian ceremonies.

However, too often men, women, and children are the heirs of myths about alcohol which may, even if we are not alcoholics, be damaging to our health.

Common Myths about Alcohol

Alcohol is good for chills. Not so: Alcohol makes a person feel warm only temporarily because the blood vessels at the surface of the skin are dilated, but as the blood is brought to the skin surface, the body loses heat. Body temperature is actually lowered.

Feeling blue? A drink will cheer you up. Not so: Alcohol intensifies what a person is feeling.

Alcohol is a stimulant. Not so: Alcohol acts as an anesthetic. The first drink or two dulls the consciousness and removes the inhibitions. It is the release of inhibitions that is often mistaken for stimulation. Therefore, many people say a "little drink" frees them from feeling shy among people.

Coffee and a cold shower will sober anyone up who has had too much to drink. Not so: Coffee and a cold shower will keep a person awake. Only the liver can metabolize the alcohol and nothing can hurry up the process.

Mixing different types of drinks makes a person drunk. Not so: Intoxication is caused by the ethyl alcohol present in all alcoholic beverages. What may contribute to making a person feel sick is the mixtures of additives in each type of alcohol. Some may have caramel coloring added; others may have a high sugar content, and others, flavor additives.

Beer or wine does not make a person as intoxicated as distilled spirits such as scotch or brandy. Not so: It depends on how much you drink of each. Twelve ounces of beer may have as much alcohol as one and one-half ounces of whiskey, scotch or brandy.

How Alcohol Affects the Body

Alcohol is a fast-acting drug because it is absorbed by the membranes of the digestive tract and passes immediately into the blood stream. The less food we have eaten, the quicker the alcohol can pass into the blood stream. This is why a drink after dinner is less potent than one before dinner, or why social drinkers like to nibble at pretzels and other snacks while they have cocktails.

A drink gulped down rather than slowly sipped will make the consumer act drunker because it is absorbed faster, and the effects will last longer. The same amount drunk slowly will not make the consumer feel as drunk even though in the end, the drinker will have the same amount of alcohol in the body as the one who drank fast. The slow drinker gives his body a chance to handle the alcohol.

Once the alcohol is in our blood stream, it is circulated throughout the body. This is how alcohol reaches the brain. Alcohol acts directly on the brain and changes its ability to work. Alcohol puts part of the brain to sleep, which naturally affects the ability of the drinker to think and make decisions. If more alcohol is consumed, the drinker can't walk a straight line or drive a car. Her speech may become slurred and the drinker may also have trouble focusing the eyes.

As the alcohol in the blood stream passes through the lungs, some of it evaporates into the air and is exhaled. One can "smell the alcohol on the breath." The other method of ridding the body of alcohol is through the kidneys, where urine is constantly being made. A tiny amount may be excreted through sweat.

However, about 90% of the alcohol in the body leaves by oxidation. Here the liver plays a major role. The alcohol enters the liver via the blood stream. In the liver, chemical changes take place, known as oxidation of alcohol. The liver can only oxidize a certain amount of alcohol each minute. A person weighing 150 pounds can manage about seven grams of pure alcohol per hour. Wine, beer or scotch—it isn't what we drink that counts, but the amount of alcohol it contains. This is why people are advised to drink slowly since the body can only manage a limited amount of alcohol. For example, if a person drinks two ounces of alcohol during the course of an hour, at the end of the hour, the alcohol in the body has passed its peak and begun to decline, but with the next drink, it starts rising again.

Depending on what one drinks, the oxidation of alcohol produces calories. One ounce of alcohol can contain as much as 163 calories. One and one-half ounces of whiskey or gin contains approximately 105 calories. Unfortunately, these calories contain no vitamins.

WOMEN AND ALCOHOL: SOME EMERGING DISCOVERIES

Alcohol is a complicated drug, and doctors are discovering new facts all the time. Some researchers are beginning to feel that women may become more easily intoxicated than men.

Tests have been made on how alcohol affects women. The principal persons behind these tests were Ben Morgan Jones, Ph.D., and his wife, Marilyn K. Jones, both of the University of Oklahoma Health Sciences Center. (Author's note: the address in Oklahoma is no longer valid. Marilyn K. Jones is deceased and Ben Morgan Jones, Ph.D. can now be reached at Ben Morgan Jones Ph.D. 2633 Broad Ave Altoona PA 16601. (814)-946-1423.) In these tests, both men and women received alcohol according to their weight. A man or woman who weighs two hundred pounds would receive twice as much alcohol in this test as a woman or a man who weighs one hundred pounds. Shortly after finishing the drink, the subjects began their alcohol breath tests using the same type of instrument commonly used by police departments throughout the country.

In judging the results of these tests, we must continually keep in mind that only small groups of less than fifty male and female volunteer social drinkers were involved. Nevertheless, these tests are important because they give us insight into the different ways alcohol may affect women.

For example, women were less capable than men on chores that require rapid reactions. When both men and women were told how and when to push a certain button after drinking, the women could not push the buttons as rapidly as the men although before drinking there was no significant difference in their performances.

Each time alcohol was administered, regardless of the dose, the women became more intoxicated than the men. The women had absorbed the alcohol faster than the men and had become intoxicated sooner.

This may have to do with the water in our bodies. Men have in their total body weight approximately ten percent more water than women. Since alcohol is distributed throughout the body in proportion to the water content of the body tissues, the alcohol tends to be more diluted in the bodies of men than in women.

The basic difference between women and men is that women have more fatty tissues and men have more muscle tissues. More water is contained in muscle tissues than fatty tissues. Therefore, when men and women who weigh the same drink equal amounts of alcohol, the men are apt to be less affected by alcohol than the women. Naturally, there are variables. An obese man may have more fatty tissues than a lean woman of the same weight.

Those women who were at their premenstrual time became more intoxicated than the other women. Evidently a woman's changing sex hormone levels may be related to the effect alcohol has on her. Feeling different reactions to alcohol at different times of the month may make a female social drinker instinctively more careful with her drinking than a male.

The researchers felt that, since men in general have a more stable hormonal level, they may be more confident about the amount of alcohol they can "hold" when they drink. This difference may make women more careful. This may be one of the reasons that women become heavy drinkers at a later age than men.

As the breathalyzer was administered again and again, it was found that the alcohol remained significantly longer in the body of those women taking the birth control pill. These results indicate that the pill may slow down the disappearance rate of alcohol from the body. And, interestingly enough, those taking the birth control pill reported drinking significantly less alcohol the previous month than those not taking the pill.

First Stages of Alcoholism

For some people, whether man or woman, drinking is a problem. Problem drinkers cause unhappiness and embarrass family and friends. Some problem drinkers—but not necessarily all—become alcoholics.

Even though there is now a suspicion that alcohol may affect women differently than men, and, even though we know that the attitudes of many women toward drinking and their early experiences with alcohol may differ from the men's, the basic definition for alcoholism is the same for both sexes.

Today alcoholics are generally regarded as being very sick people. The alcoholic is as sick as someone who has cancer, heart disease or TB. And, like cancer, heart disease or TB, alcoholism is a disease that can be recognized and arrested. If alcoholism is not arrested, it can cause permanent debilitation or premature death.

Most alcoholics start out with the same intentions as the non-alcoholic: to have no more than one or two drinks. The non-alcoholic or so-called social drinker can stop when she chooses. The alcoholic cannot and drinks herself senseless. Alcoholism is a creeping, progressive disease. Alcoholics, especially in the early stages, may go without a drink for days and weeks, but when they drink, they are problem drinkers.

No one consciously starts out drinking to become an alcoholic. Drinking may start as a pleasant activity—as a social drink to make friends, or to feel sophisticated among friends, to help celebrate a birthday, or a family anniversary. Some women drink to keep their husbands company. They may have a drink before dinner at home or when they go out together with his business friends. Other women enjoy an occasional drink at a bar or restaurant when they meet with their girl friends for a night out. In all this social process, some discover pharmacological effects.

Some may discover that drinks smother an insecurity, quiet an inexplicable nagging anxiety, or relax them after a day's work and, wonder of wonders, they don't need a doctor's prescription or his supervision as they would for tranquilizers. They can drink as much as they want.

One woman alcoholic whom we will call Mary explained how she drank without even remotely guessing that she could possibly be an alcoholic.

"I never drank much until I got married. My husband lived about 100 miles from my home town. I didn't feel comfortable with his friends. I had nothing in common with the other wives who seemed so much more capable, worldly, and prettier than anyone I had ever met. I found that when I was in this group drinks relaxed me.

"Once in a while the thought occurred to me that I was drinking a lot. Too many times I was losing my power to stop drinking after one or two drinks. I still didn't think that anything was wrong because there were periods of weeks and months when I did not drink. I usually did not drink when I went home to visit my parents, and when I did drink among my own parents and friends, I held my liquor well. However, I did drink often at home when I had to deal with complications such as having to arrange a fancy dinner party or when I lost an argument with my husband. I would, at that point, gulp alcohol and never worked out the consequences of what this drinking would do to me.

"When I think back to my drinking days, the reasons I gave for drinking seemed so trivial. I was using my emotions as a rationalization to drink. I needed a sedative for everything, for my sleepless nights, the piled up laundry, our noisy neighbors. Any excuse would do to drink."

Mary's story is similar to that of many other alcoholics who are in the first stages of alcoholism. Other alcoholics give other reason for starting to drink. It may be a loss of a parent through death or a husband through divorce. It may be the frustration of being tied down to small children and not being able to express her talent. In fact the reasons are limitless.

Patterns of Heavy Drinking

Heavy drinkers develop, consciously and unconsciously, patterns to accommodate their need for alcohol, and their personalities change to accommodate their drinking.

THE DRINKING WOMAN: REVISITED

Mary would prefer to stay by herself so that she could drink unobserved. She had a few "extras" before her husband came home for dinner or before friends came to visit. Mary showed a marked preference for heavy-drinking people. Her husband noticed she would be extremely silent and depressed or very gay and loud. She was forgetful. She would not remember when her menstrual period was due. She wasn't sure if she had had her period or might be pregnant, or if she was irregular due to her bad diet and drinking. She would forget doctors' appointments.

Deep down, Mary was frightened by her heavy drinking and by the anxiety that accompanied it. She promised herself that she would not drink so much with her husband at cocktail time or when they went out with friends.

She didn't. She drank before her husband came home and before parties. Her husband, who had grown progressively worried about Mary's drinking, was pleased that he did not see her drink anymore.

Mary discovered at parties that a few quick gulps in the bathroom soothed her for about two hours. Alcohol reduced Mary's psychomotor activity level and made her feel relaxed and tranquil. Alcohol is one of the sedative drugs, all of which are addicting. Unfortunately, this sedative effect is followed by an agitation effect, making the drinker more tense and anxious than before drinking. At that tense moment, Mary would simply disappear in the bathroom again to have a few more gulps to calm her.

Non-alcoholics who may on rare occasions also drink a little too much experience this agitative effect after the sedation wears off, but they do not drink more alcohol at that point.

Mary needed more and more drinks. She staked her bottles out around the house so that she could get at them easily and secretly. She had one bottle in the kitchen in an old pot she didn't use anymore and another one upstairs in her bedroom closet. She hid her bottles because it helped her to deny to herself and to others the amount of drinking she was doing. She thought she had a moral problem. She still did not acknowledged that she was ill. When she was not drinking, all she could think about was when she would have the next drink.

There was another change in Mary, too. Mary isolated herself from her parents. She didn't bother to travel the hundred miles anymore to visit her parents. She preferred to stay home and drink.

In desperation, her husband confided to a close friend, "I don't understand what is going on in my life. Mary doesn't have a job, yet the house is a mess when I come home. There is never any food in the house, yet the checking account is empty. I know she doesn't spend the money on clothes because she looks a mess. Mary is often asleep at six in the evening. When we go to parties, she is embarrassingly loud or extremely silent. If I try to discuss with her last night's behavior, she doesn't know what I'm talking about

"I bought her a new car for her birthday and it is more in the repair shop for dents than in use."

Alcoholism Observed

The occurrences Mary's husband mentions are all a part of the patterns of alcoholism. An alcoholic will spend all her money on liquor. She may be so busy drinking and so sick from the effects of alcohol that she may forget to bathe herself and to dress properly. When she is in such a condition, her husband can't bring himself to sleep with her. Unless he understands that she is ill, he feels she is drinking because "she doesn't love me." Mary's behavior eventually may affect her family's mental health. They may blame themselves for her behavior. They may argue continually with her about her actions. They may know that she is drinking but not connect their difficulties with her drinking. Or, they may just deny the fact that drinking is a problem in their family. If children are involved, it affects their well-being, too. This is why alcoholism is called a family disease.

An additional strain is caused by the fact that the family never knows what the alcoholic may do in her anesthetized state. Will she fall asleep with her cigarette burning? Will she be in another car accident? Unfortunately, when repeated simple car dents are involved, the insurance company and the police do not routinely check to see whether alcohol may be the cause of the accidents.

"Often Mary Is Asleep at 6 in the Evening"

If Mary's husband were to discuss this statement with a doctor, he would find that this is as much a symptom of alcoholism as red spots may be a symptom of measles. Sleep when it comes to the heavy drinker is unnatural. Alcohol interferes with dreaming, which is necessary to a proper rest and well-being. Therefore, the alcoholic never feels rested and tries to sedate herself with more alcohol.

The active drinking alcoholic may at times only look as if asleep. Alcohol decreases, the function of the brain and can cause a loss of consciousness or "passing out." Too much alcohol can paralyze the respiratory center of the brain and cause not only unconsciousness but death. However, when a person drinks frequently enough, and in large enough quantities, the brain becomes adapted to alcohol so that large amounts may be taken without unconsciousness or death ensuing.

The family of the alcoholic should be aware that other conditions in conjunction with alcohol can cause a person to pass out. Sleeping pills or tranquilizers, since their effect lasts longer when mixed with alcohol, can cause the alcoholic to pass out. Such a pass out might be very serious even if the alcoholic is used to alcohol.

Furthermore, certain metabolic conditions as diabetes or cirrhosis can cause unconsciousness even without alcohol. And the problem can be greatly aggravated by the use of large amounts of alcohol.

"The Next Day She Doesn't Know What I'm Talking About"

When Mary's husband seeks help about his wife's alcoholism, he will learn that not remembering, commonly called a blackout, is another symptom of alcoholism that the family and the alcoholic need to understand. It is a temporary loss of memory due to drinking. When a person drinks heavily and steadily and her brain becomes adapted to alcohol, she does not become unconscious as quickly as the nonalcoholic. She may even act sober. But she will have periods of time during which she has a loss of memory.

Sometimes the alcoholic will even try to cover up for the loss of memory because it is embarrassing, Usually the loss of memory is so total that she may deny the events took place.

Naturally, unless those who live with the alcoholic understand what blackouts are, they will think the alcoholic is lying and denying on purpose.

"Mary Hides Her Bottles"

Such women as Mary, who become addicted to alcohol, have an easy time hiding their drinking because as "supported" women, they have the prerogative to stay home to do chores. In the early stages of alcoholism, they use the excuse that little sips of beer or wine or sherry help them through the boring household chores. In such cases, solitary drinking is a symptom of alcoholism (this is not to be confused with the single person who has an occasional beer by herself in front of the TV).

Even women alcoholics who work tend to drink alone more so than men alcoholics. This may be, in part, because in our society, it was frowned upon for a woman to drink at lunch, and not so long ago, she was not served alcohol in restaurants when unescorted. Is it any wonder then, that if working, she will drink secretly whereas a man, even if he is an alcoholic, will have cocktails with other men? She may drink on the evenings she spends alone. At big parties she will drink privately in the bathroom. If Single, she will drink alone after work.

On skid row where the male derelicts stick together, women tend to drink alone. Many who drink in public do so because they don't have an apartment or house offering them the space and privacy to drink alone. Often in a bar she will sit in a corner away from everyone. Only a free drink would get her talking to others in the bar.

It is not easy for the alcoholic to give up drinking. The alcohol relieves momentarily the continual unpleasant feelings with which she is bothered. She feels tense, angry, ashamed of her drinking and guilty. When people comment about her drinking or try to take away her drink, she may get angry or withdraw.

The alcoholic is frightened by all these symptoms and alcohol helps her to forget her fear. Secretly, she may have tried to soothe herself by taking sedatives and tranquilizers. She may become so desperate that she may mix tranquilizers with alcohol.

Many alcoholics do not go to their physicians for normal checkups because they do not want the physician to recognize their drinking. Such alcoholics may then develop conditions that have nothing to do with alcoholism. It may be something as simple as failing to get a new prescription for a pair of eye glasses or it may be a matter of life and death such as not obtaining treatment for a case of venereal disease, or not having a yearly pap smear.

Effects of Chronic Alcohol Abuse

Unless alcoholism is discovered in the very early stages, it takes its toll on the body. Heavy drinkers don't absorb vitamin B very well and often have to get shots to compensate for the deficiency. The vitamin B12 complex is the first to be destroyed by alcohol.

Alcoholics may feel energetic after drinking since alcohol is highly caloric but has little nutritive value. The end result is malnutrition.

The liver may be severely damaged by alcohol abuse. After heavy intake of alcohol, it may become enlarged. It ordinarily returns to its original size if drinking is discontinued and a special diet is maintained. However, in a small percentage of alcohol abusers, cirrhosis, a more serious ailment of the liver, may develop. Although anyone can develop cirrhosis, 85% to 90% of deaths caused by cirrhosis are alcohol-related.

Alcohol abuse over a period of time may result in irritation of the stomach lining. In chronic abusers, the acid produced by the alcohol may burn a hole through the lining, resulting in ulcer-like damage.

Eventually, alcohol abuse can produce damaged eye muscles, permanently alter a person's gait and balance and affect mental capacity.

As the drinking progresses, so do the possibilities of body damage. For instance, people who drink become more susceptible to infection. They may develop pneumonia, TB or bronchial asthma.

In extremely severe cases, the alcoholic may become immobilized.

Since the alcohol reaches the nerves, too, the legs may lose all power of action. In severe cases, there will be an absence of ankle jerk and reflexes. Muscle damage may create a calf muscle tenderness and weakness may set in. Wherever the limbs are placed, there they remain until they are moved again by the hospital attendant.

Heavy smokers fearing cancer should know that ethanol may be an irritant to the cells in our bodies. Heavy drinkers have more cancer of the mouth and throat than do social drinkers. Most heavy drinkers smoke. Alcohol alone may not necessarily cause cancer, but it may in some way that is not yet clear, speed up the carcinogenic effects of tobacco smoke.

The note of hope is that when the alcoholic stops drinking, many of these damages can be arrested or reversed. Alcoholism can be arrested once we recognize its symptoms and are willing to admit that it is a disease and not just a moral question of will power as so many unfortunately still believe it to be.

The danger signals are clear. Do you know someone who:
1. Says she drinks to calm her nerves.
2. Says she drinks because it is the only way she feels comfortable with her friends.
3. Says she drinks to relieve feelings of boredom, depression and loneliness.
4. Says she drinks because she can't sleep.
5. Says she drinks because it helps her get her work done.
6. Says she can't remember what she said or did while she drank.
7. Hides her alcohol.
8. Refuses to discuss her drinking.
9. Has been in unusual accidents such as falling down stairs while drinking.

If you know a woman who lives this desperate life, take action.

UPDATES
- Internists, psychologists and other helping agencies screening for alcoholism frequently like to use the CAGE questionnaire, the name of which is an acronym of its four questions. It is a widely used method of screening for alcoholism.

    Two "yes" responses indicate the possibility of alcoholism. The questionnaire asks the following questions:

    Have you ever felt you needed to Cut down on your drinking?
    Have people Annoyed you by criticizing your drinking?

Have you ever felt Guilty about drinking?
Have you ever felt you needed a drink first thing in the morning (Eye-opener) to steady your nerves or get rid of a hangover?

- Women reach "bottom" faster than men
- "Telescoping" is the term used for how a woman's substance abuse disorder magnifies itself. It refers to the fact that a woman's drinking problems advances more rapidly than a man's and she may therefore be in treatment sooner than a man. A woman will have more medical, psychiatric and adverse social consequences than a man with severe alcohol abuse disorder.
- Women suffer physically more from alcohol than men. Women develop liver disease more quickly. Women increase their risk of breast cancer. Imaging studies have shown that women may acquire alcohol-induced brain changes sooner than men.
- Looking at various studies this author has come to the conclusion that women may start to drink more for emotional reasons than men. For example, Gilman and Abraham 2001, explored gender differences for 2 years and found that men with major depression were no more likely to develop alcohol dependence than men without depression. On the other hand women with depression were seven times more likely to become alcohol dependent than women without depression.
- Treatment studies report that female alcoholics have higher rates of anxiety, depression, eating disorders and borderline personality disorder, whereas men show higher rates of antisocial personality disorder.
- Serotonin is a neurotransmitter or put more directly, a chemical that which transmits our nerve impulses. Our nerve impulses relate to our sleep, depression, memory, and other neurological processes. Researchers have noted that people with an imbalance of serotonin might drink to coun-

teract this drawback. One study (Nishizawa et al) suggested that women seem to have lower rate of serotonin than men which may indicate why women become more easily depressed than men.
- Research done in 2013 by Prof. Marco Leyton of McGill University's Department of Psychiatry suggests that people at high risk for alcohol-use problems showed, while drinking, a greater dopamine response in a brain pathway that increases the desire for rewards when compared to people who are at low risk for alcohol-use problems. The dopamine is a brain neurotransmitter governing, among other areas in our body, our emotions including pleasure gratification. Heavy drinkers with low dopamine may try to stimulate their pleasure center with alcohol.
- Because psychotherapy influences biological activity in the brain (Etkin et al.) therapy and group therapy as well as associations such as Alcoholics Anonymous help to restrain addiction.
- Researchers have noted that thrill seekers are less afraid to drink heavily.
- There are a multitude of studies disclosing that adolescents (both boys and girls) with problematic temperaments such as troublesome conduct, attention deficit, anxiety and mood disorders are in danger of abusing alcohol. One summary of these complications (Underage Drinking, National Institute on Alcohol Abuse and Alcoholism (NIAAA), 2006) noted that "—research shows that the serious drinking problems (including what is called alcoholism) typically associated with middle age actually begin to appear much earlier, during young adulthood and even adolescence. Other research shows that the younger children and adolescents are when they start to drink, the more likely they will be to engage in behaviors that harm themselves and others. For example, frequent binge drinkers (nearly 1 million high school students nationwide) are more likely to engage in risky behaviors, including using other drugs such as marijuana and

cocaine, having sex with six or more partners, and earning grades that are mostly Ds and Fs in school—."
- Some schools have programs that identify high risk youngsters and encourage them to join their Peer Group Connection which basically teaches them smart life skills and how to pass those skills on to fellow students. Helping to teach other students what they have learned gives them confidence in their capabilities.

CHAPTER 3

YOU'RE JUST LIKE YOUR PARENTS— MAYBE?

Is it possible to inherit alcoholism? Since alcoholism runs in families, many alcoholics have asked and keep asking this question.

Alcoholics tend to feel very strongly about this subject even though they have nothing more solid on which to base their feelings than their personal experience and impressions. There are among the alcoholics themselves almost two teams: those who are convinced that alcoholism will someday be proven hereditary; and those who say the whole problem is one of family stress and the influence of our environment.

Consider the case of Jane, who firmly believes that alcoholism is hereditary. Jane never knew her mother and father. When she was three weeks old, she was adopted by the Jones family. Her adopted family, the Joneses, had two children, a boy and a girl, older than Jane. Both Mr. and Mrs. Jones drank socially.

Years later, when Jane married, she had a drinking problem. Her adopted brother and sister did not have a drinking problem. Jane was then told by the Joneses that her father too, had had a drinking problem.

Jane said, "I know I inherited my drinking problem. I know because there are other known case histories very similar to my own."

Jane is at least partly right. There have been some studies done on children of alcoholics. But no one has been able to prove anything conclusively.

The two most talked about studies are by Dr. M. A. Schuckit and Dr. Don Goodwin. The latter studied 55 men while the former studied 60 men and only 9 women. Both studies dealt with children born of an alcoholic parent who, like Jane, had been taken away from her biological parents at less than six weeks of age. The results showed clearly that children of alcoholic parents were apt to have more problems than those not born of alcoholic parents.

Dr. Goodwin has, as this book is going to press, completed another study of fifty women who came from homes where it was known that one parent is an alcoholic. All fifty, at a very young age, were placed with foster parents. All the data has not yet been compiled. However, preliminary readings indicate that there were tendencies for increased alcoholism among the women who had an alcoholic parent, although the rate is not as dramatic as among the men.

But does this prove that men are more apt to inherit alcoholism and that women are less apt to inherit alcoholism? There are doctors who do believe that (according to these studies) this is indeed the case. Still, one must ask what influence these parents may have had on their children in even this short length of time. How much did genetics contribute, and how much was nurtured while the child was in the mother's womb?

Alcoholics who believe that alcoholism is hereditary point to certain vulnerable groups. Such non-Europeans as the Indians, Eskimos and urban blacks, who consider themselves oppressed minorities, seem to have never experienced alcoholism until they were introduced to European patterns of drinking. Now drinking problems are prevalent in most of these minority communities. But even this is not conclusive. It may still be asked whether there were present genetic factors which became active in the presence of alcohol.

The Irish see their alcohol problem from another viewpoint. They say that alcohol in Ireland was used as a drug to help them face such problems as hunger, poverty, and late marriages. The church frowned on sex out of wedlock. Most farms could support only one family at a time. The children too had often to wait for the parents to die until they could afford to marry. Drinking, commonly called the Irish virus, was an approved alternative. It was considered a proper manifestation of masculinity. We do not know how the women dealt with this stress. Were they high strung? Did they drink secretly? Unfortunately, for the most part women have been conveniently left out of most of what has been written about the Irish virus. What has been asked is: Was the Irish virus transmitted through tradition, genetically, or both?

No gene up to now has been labeled "alcoholism" in the same way, for instance, that the dominant gene for "brown eyes" has been identified. There is speculation, though, that some people may be more genetically predisposed to heavy drinking than others. No one knows what it is exactly that enables some people to develop a physical tolerance to alcohol or what causes them to crave alcohol until they become physically dependent on it. Those people whose physical nature does not permit them to "enjoy" more than one or two drinks are not in danger of becoming an alcoholic. Such people, after more than two drinks, get sleepy, throw up, feel incapacitated, hate the taste, find the physical discomfort so great that it does not make them "feel good" or soothe any fears.

Is there a genetically determined difference in drug effect? Does the liver act faster in some people. And therefore permit less alcohol to reach the central nervous system? Or, why is there a variation among people in the rate at which alcohol disappears from the blood? Why does the central nervous system in some people adapt itself to a chronic intake or addictiveness?

We will not know for many years to come, if ever in our lifetime, the answers to all the questions asked in this chapter. Nor are we the first generation to debate these questions. Indeed, it sometimes seems that we have not advanced beyond Plutarch, the ancient Greek author who observed in 66 A.D., "One drunkard begets another." It is safe to guess there were those in 66 A.D. who did not agree with Plutarch's statement, which was based on nothing more scientific than his own personal observations.

Updates
- Don W. Goodwin who was known for his research on alcoholism and heredity, and for his studies of babies of alcoholic parents adopted by non-alcoholic parents is still cited today for his work. In 1979 he concluded: "while there was no significant relationship between alcohol abuse among adoptees and the foster parents with whom they lived, there was a consistent and significantly increased risk of alcoholism in adoptees (even if adopted at birth) if a biological parent had abused alcohol. This at least suggests the possibility of a hereditary factor." In discussing heredity he pointed out that it was imperative to note that "–groups with relatively low alcoholism rates similarly may be protected by an innate sensitivity to alcohol." (such as instant sleepiness, nausea) One question is whether this sensitivity is inherited as well?
- Other physicians have noted if one is born with a predisposition to alcoholism but is never exposed to alcohol that person may in fact lead a productive life free of alcoholism.
- A summary of studies using population based twin registries presented by Carol A. Prescott, Ph.D. has found the genetic influences on alcoholism to be of similar magnitude in males and females.
- Joel Gelernter, M.D. and Henry R. Kranzler, M.D. in *The American Psychiatric Publishing Textbook of Substance Abuse Treatment 4th edition* remind those trying to understand heredity and alcoholism that there are two methods, often used together, that can be used to identify the risks of heredity. One is the study of the entire genome (our genes) and the other is the use of statistical (rather than biological) methods of conclusion. In their explanation they cite the studies of children of alcoholic parents who were adopted at birth and proved to have a higher rate of alcoholism as compared to children of non-alcoholics. These latter conclusions are statistical.
- Metabolism genes influence alcohol dependence. Research has shown that some enzymes (that provide our ability to di-

gest alcohol) are encoded by different genes that determine our capacity to digest alcohol. Those who can "hold" their alcohol are in greater danger of becoming alcoholics.
- Gene-by-environment interaction refers to a combination of genetic and environmental causes that can act together, promoting alcoholism risk more than either acting alone.

CHAPTER 4

PREGNANCY

In the Old Testament an angel appears to Samson's mother, who has been unhappily barren, and says, "Behold, now thou bearest not: but thou shalt conceive and bear a son. Now, therefore beware, I pray thee and drink not wine nor strong drink and eat not any unclean things."

There are those who feel every pregnant woman could use such an angel. The pregnant woman who drinks heavily faces unique problems. She may fall and bring on a miscarriage or damage herself. She may forget to go for her regular medical checkups. She may not go out for days at a time depriving herself of the necessary fresh air and exercise. She may be so busy drinking that she forgets about taking the proper nourishment.

How Alcohol May Affect the Fetus

But the alcohol she ingests may have more direct consequences. Alcohol passes on to the fetus in the same concentration as nourishment is passed on to the fetus.

We know that excessive amounts of coffee, nicotine, or tranquilizers have an effect on the fetus. Undoubtedly, so does alcohol. These babies may be as much in danger of a withdrawal syndrome as the mother is.

In many cases women drink and there is no withdrawal syndrome. A lot has to do with how long she has been drinking, her physical make-up, and how much she drinks during pregnancy. A small group of white middle-class women in Seattle, Washington, none of whom were alcoholics, were closely questioned about their drinking habits before and during pregnancy by research workers. Many described adverse physiological effects when drinking during pregnancy. Among these were stomach irritation, a nausea reportedly brought on by drinking and not by the pregnancy itself, headaches, and a diuretic effect. In general, alcohol tasted and smelled bad to them.

Those pregnant women in the group who drank more heavily before pregnancy did not lessen their drinking quite as much as the other pregnant women in this study. The babies of the heavier drinking women weighed less but were still within the normal weight range.

Unfortunately, there has never been a study done to see if alcoholic women, when pregnant, also drink proportionately less.

Fetal Alcohol Syndrome
The fetal alcohol syndrome when it occurs is startling. Dr. David Smith at the University of Washington, School of Medicine, observed that a baby of an actively drinking alcoholic mother who had a blood test right after birth proved to be intoxicated! He observed that the amniotic fluid that had surrounded the baby of another drinking mother had an odor of ethanol. And, still another baby delivered of an alcoholic mother had ethanol on his breath!

While it is hard to obtain statistics on malformations of babies of alcoholics, there have been reports in the United States and in Europe that some babies of actively drinking women were found to have: abnormally smaller heads, limited elbow motion, heart abnormalities, and low birth weight. Some died; others suffered from alcohol withdrawal. Some had deficient I.Q.s. These studies tend to be of small groups of 10, 20, 30 mothers and often of a low socio-economic level. In most cases, the father, needless to say a gene contributor, is not mentioned. This may be because the father is unknown.

Obstetricians who discover that a patient is an alcoholic should encourage her to go into the hospital for treatment immediately. One obstetrician said openly that he encourages any actively drinking woman who refuses to be treated for her alcoholism to have an abortion.

A prominent obstetrician in Boston said, "A baby's central nervous system could become dependent on alcohol while the mother is carrying the child. Due to the biochemical changes caused by the alcohol in the offspring's central nervous system, the child may be born jittery or hyperactive.

"I tell these mothers that not only may she be impairing the child's central nervous system, but, as she drinks, her very own central nervous system may be abused to the extent that she won't be able to care properly for the child after it is born."

Since Time Began

Any woman who is pregnant and has a drinking problem should not feel that she is unique. Nor should she feel that it is a phenomenon of our modern age. It may help her to know that each society in history has been concerned with the effect alcohol has on the infant in the mother's womb and on the milk in the mother's breast. Both ancient Carthage and Sparta had laws prohibiting the use of alcohol by newly married couples to prevent conception during intoxication. Robert MacNish of Glasgow wrote in 1827, "The children of such persons [heavy drinkers or alcoholics] are apt to be puny and emaciated. . . ." In 1834, an English committee on drunkenness stated with great concern to the house of Commons that infants born of an alcoholic mother were apt to have "a starved, shriveled and imperfect look."

We are today in an era of research, an era in which there is help for the alcoholic woman. Our laws are such that she does not have to carry the child if she does not want to. If she is alone in this world and wants to continue her pregnancy, there are (as this book will point out) countless facilities where she can seek help. Some of these facilities have live-in arrangements where she can be with other women in the same situation. These women gain strength from each other's problems and outlooks.

If she needs counseling rather than a live-in facility, she can ask her obstetrician to refer her, during this most important time of her life, to a therapist, counselor, or social worker who will help her gain courage, insight, and a proper outlook on her personal future. No woman needs to be alone at such a difficult time. Pregnancy is an emotional experience for all women, not just alcoholics.

Even a pregnant woman who is a recovered alcoholic and who does not necessarily need emotional support outside of the family should tell her doctor her drinking history. She may, for instance, need more vitamins than other women. She may have an aberrant reaction to certain drugs.

A woman should never be afraid to confide to her obstetrician her present or past drinking problems. If she does not feel comfortable talking to her doctor, she should change doctors.

Doctors want to help the alcoholic woman and prescribe the right kind of medicine for her but can only help a patient if she wants to be helped. Dr. Frank Seixas, medical director of National Council on Alcoholism wrote about all alcoholic patients in the *Annals of Internal Medicine*, "This (to help) is not necessarily easy (for the medical doctors) because although moderate drinkers will usually give reliable reports about their drinking habits, those with alcoholism commonly have a syndrome of denial that interferes with the accurate reporting of the amount of alcohol they have ingested."

Any actively drinking alcoholic woman who is pregnant, for her sake, for her child's sake, for her family's sake, should tell her doctor. The thought of living without alcohol may be frightening, but the doctor is there to help and to make you feel as comfortable as he can. This may be the beginning of a whole new life for you and your child.

UPDATES
- Women planning pregnancy or finding themselves pregnant may find it helpful to know that according to a study done of 1,969 women in Australia (published in 2013 in BJOG) most women who drank regularly before becoming pregnant continued to drink throughout their pregnancy even when healthcare guidelines promoted abstinence. The question arises here as to how the alcoholic woman who can't

control her drinking during pregnancy may be helped to arrest her drinking?
- Women who are pregnant and using alcohol are often afraid to admit to a drinking problem because they have a fear of social disapproval and legal problems such as jail, having the children who are at home and/or the new born baby taken away by social services.
- Alcoholism among pregnant women is better approached as a public health concern rather than a criminal justice issue. Caring obstetricians and gynecologists are sensitive to drinking women's needs and will help them find substance abuse treatment.
- Treatment for the addicted prisoner varies from state to state, from prison to prison. Some have ongoing Alcoholics Anonymous meetings. Quite a few of our states are becoming more knowledgeable and are enabling their judges to rule where appropriate parole with court mandated treatment.
- National Women's Law Center 11 Dupont Circle, NW, # 800 Washington, DC 20036 Telephone: (202)-588-5180 Fax: (202)-588-5185 E-mail: info@nwlc.org is devoted to women with legal questions. There are as well lawyers specializing in addiction who are prepared to help any pregnant woman with custody and treatment questions. Legal Aid provides help to those who can't afford a lawyer.
- Pregnant women who have transportation problems sometimes find it easier not to seek medical help. Public Law (102)-321-1992 specifically asks under the Substance Abuse Prevention and Treatment Block Grant that each state provide pregnant women with child care aid and transportation to health care. Those seeking more information should contact Health Resources and Services Administration's National Maternal and Child Health Clearinghouse at 1-(888)-275-4772.
- The U.S. Department of Health and Human Services has issued a patient privacy act. Ask your doctor to go over with you your privacy rights.

- According to a study reported in 2007 maternal depression is common and may increase the risk of substance abuse or a relapse of abuse during pregnancy.
- Pregnant women as well as women suffering from postpartum depression might reduce their substance abuse if they receive, under the care of a doctor, appropriate anti-depressant medication.
- A recent review revealed that pregnant women who discontinued the use of antidepressants during pregnancy had a greater likelihood of relapsing into their depression than those women who continued their antidepressants. Pregnant women need to discuss the dosage carefully with their obstetrician to be sure that the amount prescribed is safe for the mother as well as for the baby she is carrying.

CHAPTER 5

STRESS AND FAMILY LIVING

Wouldn't it be nice if with each bottle of alcohol there came a sign: Warning! It has been determined that people who drink to ease stress and emotional pain are in danger of becoming alcoholics.

Everyone at some point in life experiences stress and everyone copes differently with it. Some zero in on the problem and try to remove the stress. Some yell. Some hit. Some over-eat. Some will jog, play tennis, go to church. Others will see a psychiatrist. The alcoholic will drink.

What Is Stress?
We all think we know what stress is. Who hasn't said, "I am exhausted. What a lot of stress and pressure I had today." But few of us know what stress can do within our bodies, know how to control it or make it work in a positive way for us.

Stress is our body's mental, chemical, and physical reaction to situations that arouse, scare, endanger, excite or confuse us.

Stress can be good or bad. Jumping out of the way of an oncoming car can be stressful. Rushing to put out a fire can be stressful. Learning that we just won a thousand dollars can be stressful. Watching our youngest go off to school for the first time can be stressful. Being promoted to a position we always wanted, be it president of the local PTA or head of our department in our company, can be stressful.

Stress is intended to help us handle our problems. It warns us to be on the alert. Handled well, stress can strengthen us. When stress overwhelms us, it can cause us illness, such as hypertension or ulcers. It can cause us to seek relief in alcohol, tranquilizers and sedatives or in such philosophies as Zen, Transcendental Meditation and encounter groups. Some drugs such as alcohol might set up some physical imbalances and keep us from coping with our stresses. The examples vary greatly with the situations. If we have excessive alcohol in our system, there is a chance that our body or stress system may not react to the "oncoming car." Some of the stress reactions we experience are so subtle that we may not even notice them. Others are very noticeable. Who hasn't had a racing heart, sweated, or couldn't eat a thing when something excited or upset us?

Let's look at stress a little more closely by studying a specific stress occurrence. Mrs. Smith's young nephew, Michael, was visiting her while his parents were on a business trip. Mrs. Smith's house was on a private beach on the ocean. Mrs. Smith sat on the beach doing her needlepoint while Michael played at the ocean's edge. Mrs. Smith couldn't explain how it happened but suddenly she saw little Michael bobbing up and down in the ocean, obviously being pulled out further by the current.

Mrs. Smith bolted up with an energy she didn't know she had within her. She ran swiftly into the water, and although she had always been known as a mediocre swimmer, she now made fast and long, strong strokes. She had never had a course in life saving, but somewhere in the back of her mind, she remembered seeing pictures in a Red Cross book of how you hold a drowning person when you pull him out of the water. Luckily, Michael could swim well enough to stay afloat. Mrs. Smith had to work extra hard to get back to the shore with Michael because there was an undercurrent. They made it, but had anyone asked Mrs. Smith to swim so fast and well in the ocean for pleasure, she would have said that she was not capable of doing it under any circumstances.

How Stress Works

When Mrs. Smith saw her nephew in danger of drowning, several mechanisms in her body prepared her for the extra effort needed to save him and to protect her own body from harm. Some of these were a discharge of adrenalin-type hormones which increased her blood pressure and pulse rate. Her whole nervous system became alarmed and tense in preparation for saving little Michael. Extra sugar was pumped into her blood for extra needed energy. Her digestive system under such stress shut down so its blood supply was free to be sent to the muscles and the brain, where it was needed. Thus, she was able to think faster. Remember, Mrs. Smith was able to recall photos of life saving procedures in the Red Cross book which she ordinarily would not have recalled.

Blood supplies may also be shifted away from the skin to the needed area. This explains why, under extreme stress, we may be cold and pale. If stress continues, our mechanisms can become exhausted. In Mrs. Smith's case, that might well have resulted in her and Michael drowning.

After having lived through a stressful situation, be it physical, such as fighting an infection, or mental, such as hearing that a much-loved relative died, we feel tired. We may sleep more to restore the normal balance in our muscles and other tissues in our bodies. We may eat more to replenish the fuel that has been eaten up. If, instead of eating and resting, we drink alcohol, our body's responses to cope with such stresses or emergencies may be reduced. Furthermore, if we drink instead of nourishing and resting our bodies after we have undergone stress, our bodies would not be ready for the next stress with which life may confront us. Many alcoholics are so run down that their bodies cannot fight off a cold or pneumonia. Also, if they are drinking actively, they do not know when they feel "chilled" and do not react to protect their bodies.

Stressors

The alcoholic may help herself by looking at stress and stressors. Stress is the response of the body to the stressor. The stressor is the cause that upsets, excites, scares, or confuses us. This stressor may be extreme heat, extreme cold, illness, infection, joy, or sorrow.

For the rest of this chapter, we are going to talk about stressors that may affect the alcoholic. It is important to note that the results are not always bad. Dr. Hans Selye, a professor at the University of Montreal who first labeled stress in medical terms, likens stress to electricity: it can be used constructively (to light up a dark house) or destructively (to start a fire).

Sometimes there are factors that can exaggerate our stress. Some are social. If we live in an over-crowded tenement where the crime rate is high, we may have to deal with fear every time we come home after dark. We will look at these social stressors in greater depth in our culture chapter.

Some stressors may be environmental. If we suffer from allergies and live in an area that has heavy pollution, our body has to deal with that extra problem.

Some stress may come from our families. If we never felt loved, argued continually with our parents or felt other brothers or sisters were favored, this may cause us stress.

People Who Do Not Take Stress Well

People who do not take stress well and who are under stress may lose their perspective about how well they can handle a problem.

Sometimes if we ourselves, or someone in the family or a helper reassures us that we can find a way to solve our stress, that other people in the same situation have solved this particular problem, we do manage.

In childhood, we may have experienced anxiety in situations that are not really dangerous. These anxieties may last into adult life. Normally, neurotic symptoms of childhood disappear and are forgotten. However, if as adults we are faced with a situation that reminds us of our past failures, our neurotic symptoms may reappear. Under such conditions, we may have a nervous breakdown. The words "nervous breakdown" sound frightening, but actually can be the beginning of working out what causes our stress. A nervous breakdown may be explained in part as a condition in which we experience excessive anxiety even in situations that are really not dangerous.

Not all the stressors we experience in our youth are obvious to us because we may have found it more convenient to repress these facts and tell ourselves we had a perfect youth.

Case History: Jane T.

Jane T. had everything (or so she kept telling herself) a youngster could want. Pretty clothes, a beautifully decorated room of her own and glamorous summer trips with her mother. Jane said, "My mother really, really cared."

Jane's mother over-protected her. When Jane, as a teenager, had difficulties in school with a teacher, it was her mother who went to the school to talk for Jane. When Jane went to the movies with her friends, her mother always went along because she felt it was dangerous for the girls to be out alone. Jane's mother drank only at night, and during the day she used her energy to clean fanatically. Every closet was spick and span. She didn't belong to any organizations because she claimed the women depressed her. When out with Jane, she fantasized that strange men were looking at her with interest.

As a teenager, Jane used to come straight home from school every day because she knew her mother was waiting for her. Jane felt guilty if she left her mother alone for too long. She always had had this feeling from the time she went off to kindergarten. She also went to college near home, and afterwards, she lived at home until she got married.

Toward dinner time, her father would frequently telephone to tell them that he wouldn't be home for dinner. He was working late. Her mother used to think he had been working late too frequently, and she usually decided to have a few early cocktails.

Jane T. is now married. She hoped to have a baby; instead, she had a miscarriage. She talked to the doctor about how upset she is. In place of urging her to go to counseling, the doctor prescribed valium to help her over the difficult time. Jane feels very discouraged even with the valium, and, like her mother, she finds it helpful to have a cocktail. In this crisis, Jane is, in part, living through again a helplessness she felt when her father didn't come home and her mother got drunk. Jane was never taught to stand on her own feet and deal with a crisis.

Had Jane been encouraged to play with the neighborhood children, to choose her own friends, had she been permitted to have some unsupervised activities, had she not lived at home as a young adult, she might have been able to take her miscarriage in her stride.

Jane never understood why her father worked late. Because her mother reacted as if he might be out on the town with other women, it made Jane feel insecure about her father. It made her feel as if she had only been raised by her mother. Nothing was clear cut to Jane. Jane's youth was ambivalent. Jane felt as deserted by her father as a girl who comes from any broken home.

Another Case History: Sara

Sometimes we are very aware of the conflicts in our upbringing. Sara, a case in point, never got along with her mother. She blamed her mother for all the trouble at home. Sara did not understand that alcoholism in the home had complicated her mother's life.

Sara's mother was very different from Jane's mother. She was a very strict, cold, demanding mother. Sara's mother often lectured her about morals and nagged her about her friends. Nothing Sara ever did was good enough. In her mother's eyes, she was not pretty. Her school grades could have been better, and her mother kept reminding her that she was was too much like her father. Sara never felt that her mother bought her as many clothes as she needed. In public gatherings, her mother acted entirely different than at home. She spoke softly, kindly, and acted fluttery and helpless.

Sara loved her father, who tried to give her everything. Her father drank a lot but never scolded, never demanded, and was always ready to help Sara or anyone who asked him. Her father was very close to his aging mother, who always came over to nurse him when he had a hangover because she felt Sara's mother didn't take proper care of her son. She would always say to him, "Oh, my poor heart, your drinking aggravates me so." Sara had mixed feelings about her grandmother because the lady was overly jealous of her and of her mother and even of Sara's love for her father. Sara thought she never wanted to be like her mother, but always nice and fun-loving like her father.

Sara's parents are dead now, and she has a job in an advertising firm. Sara never married, but enjoys the company of the men in her firm, and, like them, drinks just "like a man" or, like the alcoholic her father was.

The Problems of Sara and Jane

Sara and Jane's drinking got so bad that they are both today in the same treatment center trying to straighten out their lives. Sara had never understood that when drinking, she was copying her father. Jane, by the same token, had never understood that when drinking, she was copying her mother.

Once they both admitted to themselves that they were alcoholics and that drinking was destroying their lives, they both felt that they had to look at their pasts to see what started them on the road to alcoholism.

Sara and Jane, although their lives were very different, would find a common denominator in the lack of security of their homelife. Both Sara and Jane felt respectively that one parent was nicer than the other. Both felt that each had one jealous parent. Sara felt her mother was jealous of her relationship with her father. Jane felt her mother was jealous of her father's relationship with the outside world. Both felt that their fathers did not "praise" each of their mothers, and by the same token, their mothers did not approve of each of their father's lifestyle. Both remember their parents arguing about how to raise their children and that their parents did not agree on religion. Such negative family patterns play a significant part in making a girl feel insecure in her future role as a woman, and thus adds to her chances of becoming an alcoholic.

An alcoholic rather than seek help for her excessive anxiety may choose to drink and thereby intensify a situation that could be cleared up.

Family Background

Adult women experience countless stresses, and if they did not learn as children a way to handle stressful situations, they may feel lost.

For some reason unknown to therapists, women more so than men tend to come from homes where there has already been a history of alcoholism or some form of psychiatric disorder. Dr. Albert N. Browne-Mayers, Associate Medical Director of National Council on Alcoholism, says that we don't know how much of female passivity is due to the culture factor and how much is.due to inherited female traits. He reminds us that there is (also) a tendency in our culture for girls to be taught to be passive to circumstances while boys are encouraged to tackle all aspects of life. Fortunately, Dr. Browne-Mayers feels, this is changing.

These disorders and stresses that these women saw at home may include:

A close relative who suffered from alcoholism.
A close relative who tried to commit suicide.
A close relative who did commit suicide.
A close relative who has had trouble with the law.

Having lived through these stresses without having been taught to cope, some women are like a "sunburned person"—the slightest problem that wouldn't hurt the unscathed person becomes magnified.

If the distress is strong enough, it may lead to suicide. Twice as many women as men engage in suicidal gestures. There are many reasons for suicide. She may have such extreme anger at the people who have hurt her in a real or imaginary way that she may want to punish them by killing herself. "Just wait until I am gone. They'll miss me."

She may have such guilt feelings that she may want to punish herself. Or, she may feel momentarily so hopeless that she may decide at that moment to end it all. Doctors have noted that women are more likely to commit or contemplate suicide immediately before or after their periods. If a woman uses alcohol to cope with premenstrual difficulties, anger, or hopelessness, it may intensify all these feelings and lead her to commit suicide.

Life Crisis

Therapists in discussing drinking with women alcoholics have noticed that women will often pinpoint the start of their drinking to a very specific stress in their lives. This observation is supported by at least two studies on drinking by women. In 1957 Edith Lisansky noted that all the women studied in an outpatient clinic attributed the onset of heavy drinking to specific life crises similar to the ones listed below. Joan Curlee in 1970 stated that female drinking is often precipitated by a "middle-age identity crisis," such as the death of a husband, divorce, or menopause.

Many of the family problems may be no more than the natural rhythm of our life cycle. Some of these problems we will discuss in greater depth in our discussion of sex.

Some of the more common reasons given for starting to drink are:

"I started to drink when:
    I gave up my career to have children.
    The demands of small children were too much.
    The strains of marital troubles were too much.
    I had in-law problems.
    My youngest started school.
    I was living by myself.
    I was bored.
    I needed to escape drabness and poverty.
    I had a miscarriage.
    My parent died and I went to pieces.
    I learned that I was infertile.
    I had an operation on the uterus or ovaries.

I suffered post partum depression.
I was in menopause.
I had an abortion.
My husband divorced me.
As a senior citizen who had lost her husband, loneliness was too much for me."

Family Relationships

Some counselors and therapists who are trying to make their patients aware of what made them use alcohol to cope with the stressors in their lives are asking each new person in their treatment centers to fill in a questionnaire that asks them to examine their relationships at home. Therapists feel, for example, that it is very important to know whether a woman feels another sibling was more favored than she, whether another sibling received a better education than she. Did she have anyone in her family in whom she could confide? How did she feel about her mother, father? Does she herself feel intelligent, pretty, and appealing?

While these questions are of interest to all of us, even to those of us who have no debilitating problems, it is very dangerous to analyze ourselves. We need an objective person such as a therapist to help us interpret our problems. Many a person has gone into therapy and talked and talked about how someone hurt her, only to find out that it was something entirely different that caused her problems. She may have been talking and talking to avoid the true question of pain.

Each one of us deals differently with our stressors. We are all individuals. To portray how we all vary, let's look closely at how four different women reacted to a father. The first patient chose to drink like daddy. The second patient felt her mother never understood her alcoholic father. The patient married an alcoholic and tried to treat him better than her mother had treated her daddy. Instead, she drank as much as her husband and became an alcoholic herself. The third patient after much therapy learned that she may have had such a "good" relationship with her daddy that no man she marries can live up to him. The fourth patient could not understand why she married someone so completely different from her father. Her therapist told her she may have loved her father so deeply that she is subconsciously afraid of getting too close to him, and may pick someone who is exactly the opposite.

These are only a few variables of what could be the result of a father complex.

Security or good mental health cannot be defined in one chapter or in a few case histories. Nor can everything be focused on our family life. How we and our families interacted in our communities is very important.

Community Status

People who have worked with alcoholics say how we feel while growing up in our town may have a lasting effect on us. If we felt poorer, less well-dressed than the rest, or even more over-indulged or over-privileged than other youngsters, it can make us feel at a disadvantage and just as under-privileged. Sometimes these feelings haunt us for the rest of our lives. This is especially true if we felt isolated from our teachers, our community, and our schoolmates. Such women will tell you, "I never took part in school activities," "I did not feel that the teachers approved of me even if I kept up in my work," "I just felt different from the other children in school, and I wondered whether the children in school felt that I and my family were different."

When a woman lacks confidence as a teenager, she may drink to give herself confidence. Once a glass of alcohol or a beer can is in someone's hands who feels she is a flat-chested, ugly duckling and a dull conversationalist, she becomes momentarily, in her own mind, a good-looking woman and a fantastic conversationalist.

Many teenagers, even those who have a healthy makeup, may feel insecure about their personalities, looks, and themselves. It is part of their developmental pattern. When alcohol is used to help these insecurities, it may become a crutch that too often remains for life.

Where Did We Learn to Drink?

When we are young, we learn many things unconsciously. How our parents or a favorite aunt or uncle drank may have influenced us. Who did we choose for a model? Did we decide on our own that we "needed" a drink to cope with our stresses? Probably not. When this question of "where did we learn to drink?" was brought up in a treatment center, one woman related the following story:

"There never had been an alcoholic in our family. Both Mom and Dad worked. On weekends, we didn't do too much together because Mom and Dad were usually tired. During the week, Mom placed me in the home of a sitter. It seemed like the perfect solution since the sitter's house was within walking distance of my school. Aunt Marge, as I called her, was warm and loving. Her children were grown and she was a widow. Aunt Marge sipped sherry all day long. She managed well while she drank. I guess I learned to drink from Aunt Marge, who I loved more than my mom."

The other extreme, being taught that all drinking is evil and wicked, may have an equally adverse effect on a human being. A child who comes from a home where all drinking is forbidden may react strongly and adversely to the family's teetotalism. Of course, it does depend on why the family doesn't drink. Some people don't drink because they don't enjoy it. They may have an allergic reaction or a condition such as diabetes or sinus which does not permit them to drink. But, if she feels her parents didn't permit drinking because of religion, or the fear that "drink in itself is 'evil,'" she may rebel. At first she may want to experiment with alcohol. Alcohol may represent freedom to her, especially if the men in the family were encouraged to drink and the women were told to "mind their place." She may try it to see if it helps her to have fun. She may want to have a social drink at parties to show that she belongs to the group. Some teenagers get into a fast crowd or a crowd who wants to say to the world, "We dare anything." However, if she never saw any drinking at home, she will find it difficult to distinguish between healthy and unhealthy drinking patterns. Since she wasn't permitted to drink at home, she may feel guilty when she has her first drink out of the house. She may drink more to allay her feeling of guilt.

A girl who saw her parents or a parent drink to cope with everyday stress, or who saw her parents drink every night until they fell asleep, will also not know how to drink. Such a girl, without realizing it, may use the same drinking technique when she is with her friends. Such youngsters who had difficulties as teenagers in choosing the right peer relations and in feeling secure in their friendships may continue to have these problems in adult life. These people may, like their parents, choose alcohol to make themselves feel better.

One woman who is not an alcoholic but who worked in a treatment center was once asked by her patients to tell them about her experiences with alcohol. This is what she said:

"When I was a child, my parents used to drink on festive occasions such as birthdays or anniversaries. When they had friends over for a barbecue, they used to sip these tall cold rum or gin and tonic drinks while they waited for the charcoals to warm up. If the drink looked especially good, I would ask for a sip or for the orange slice in the drink. When my parents had friends over for dinner, I used to pass the dips and the hors d'oeuvres, I never saw either of my parents drink alone or act drunk. The first time I was offered a drink at a friend's house—I remember we were sixteen and a group of us had gathered together to plan a party—I drank that beer as casually as I had had those sips at my parents' barbecue. I didn't feel guilty that we were drinking even though we were under the legal age, nor did I have a great urge to finish the can of beer in my hand. As I remember it, it was a fun evening and the fun on my part wasn't dependent on the beer."

This woman is obviously not in danger of becoming an alcoholic. Drink for her is a social function. She sees no adventure in drinking. She does not see it as something that will make her popular, witty, bright, beautiful, or heroic. She sees it for what it is—alcohol.

Once the drinking woman knows what stressors can do to her, and recognizes that she may be using alcohol and other drugs to cope with these stressors, she is in a position to make stress work for her rather than against her.

Alcoholics Anonymous, a self-help group, answers this question partly by what many call their hardest step in their program. All alcoholics are asked to take a searching inventory of themselves. This does not only include our past, but also our present life.

Unknowingly, our culture may be causing us stress. We may be drinking to block out hunger, cold, and an ugly environment. We may not know where we belong because we come from a fragmented culture. Perhaps we believe in being a "liberated woman," but our parents or husbands, for whatever reason they may have, don't want us to be what we would like to be. Or, perhaps we feel society doesn't understand our sexual being.

It can be a hundred and one things. We may be concerned about our children's life styles. We may, at the moment, be experiencing an unhappy marriage. We are going to look at some of these problems in greater depth. And, once we know that there could be positive alternatives and reactions to all our stressors, our motivation can change from "needing a drink" to "wanting to do my own constructive thing."

Updates
- Counselors working with active alcoholics worry if alcohol has distorted the patient's memory. George E. Vaillant in his book, *The Natural History of Alcoholism Revisited*, explains the problem quite elegantly, "But just as light passing through water confounds our perceptions, the illness of alcoholism profoundly distorts the individual's personality, his social stability, and his own recollection of relevant childhood variables."
- According to a study done by Greenfield and O'Leary, women tend to explain their drinking as a consequence to their mood or anxiety and not as the primary problem.
- Psychiatrists treating women alcoholics find it helpful sometimes to prescribe selective serotonin reuptake inhibitors (SSRIs), because they can ease symptoms of moderate to severe depression. Much research still needs to be done on which medication is beneficial and what dosage an alcoholic needs.
- Doctors S. F. Greenfield and G. Hennessy point out that "Patients often feel great relief when they are asked questions about their condition because . . . [the clinician] can understand what the experience of the condition might be like, and may be able to offer the patient relief through some form of treatment".

- Drinking alcohol will make any stressful situation worse because it prevents the alcoholic from thinking clearly and may therefore cause her to make poor decisions.
- Moving to a new location may be helpful if the present location continues to evoke stress and anxiety. For example, Judy, age 16, was attending a high school where drinking and drugs were part of her friends' social scene. After spending a summer in rehabilitation Judy wanted to be with her friends again. She felt stressed and anxious if she was not with her friends. Her parents understood that they had to get Judy away from her established social scene. Her mother's sister offered to let Judy attend high school in her town if she signed an agreement that she would attend AA and make friends with classmates who did not drink.
- Women who are stressed because of posttraumatic syndrome such as rape, threats and other abuses might drink to cover up their discomfort. Some studies have revealed that women may suppress their posttraumatic syndrome and years later when their stress, hurt, or pain can no longer be repressed they drink and/or take drugs. Doctors recommend that any such hurt not be permitted to fester and be treated by a therapist.
- Kessler et al reported in 1996 that the National Comorbidity Study (comorbidity refers to more than one medical condition such as anxiety and alcoholism) revealed that 86% of alcohol dependent women they studied had as well another psychiatric disorder.
- It is essential to think what is going on in your life the moment you pick up that drink. Are you dealing with a memory? What are you feeling—stress, anxiety?
- Studies have shown that, for women who seek adventure, sensations such as "Lets all go out and get drunk!" are associated with a higher risk of alcoholism.

CHAPTER 6

THE ALCOHOLIC WOMAN IN THE UNHEALTHY MARRIAGE

In this chapter, we are dealing not so much with sex as with the attitudinal relationship between a husband and his alcoholic wife. Each marriage is unique. Each marriage reacts differently to the conflicting emotions that alcoholism evokes. While the drinking is or was active, maladjustments may form in the marriage. Years of compulsive drinking may have evoked emotional change in both partners. Because there is a development of relationship when two people live together, all marriages, not just alcoholic marriages, change with the years.

The list of possible relationship developments is endless. A husband may be emotionally dependent on his wife to make him feel wanted. The woman may need a husband to make her feel feminine. A woman may become very dependent on her husband to support her and their children. Others, as the children are growing up, may take courses, do volunteer work, or build up a career and thus, become autonomous. This presupposes that the non-alcoholic woman's health is so sufficient that she can make such choices in her marriage.

The alcoholic woman, until she decides to stop drinking, has no such choices. When drunk, she can't understand what is happening.

THE DRINKING WOMAN: REVISITED

The alcoholic woman is reduced to a child-like state. She is very dependent on her husband. When she is inebriated, she cannot manage her own life or the affairs of the family. She is not capable of driving a car, managing child care, or paying simple grocery bills.

In some cases, unbeknown to the wife, (and even unbeknown to himself) a husband may oppose therapy because he is using his wife's alcoholism to justify his own maladjustments and inadequacies. He is not about to encourage her to go into treatment unless he sees his own problem and is willing to end his own suffering. Rather than face up to their problems, many men prefer to undergo the painful experience of a divorce.

To the world he may act like a "long-suffering husband" who is doing his best to keep the ship from sinking. She has truly hurt his rightful male pride, as well as his home and children. He may be thinking, "I have a wife I can't control. I made a poor choice in picking a wife. She is not representative of my name. She is not taking care of *my* children."

Six Cases

Counselors' notebooks are full of case histories of marriages which, if the wives of such self-sacrificing men were sober, might not be able to go on. The following six case histories are just a few examples of patterns in a family that may keep an alcoholic woman drinking.

Case 1: The Triangle

Not uncommon is the husband with a girl friend whom he does not want to marry. A drunken wife gives him the excuse to have a girl friend. The girl friend understands that the needs of the sick wife and helpless children keep him from getting a divorce. He has probably told his girl friend that if he divorces his wife she may commit suicide.

There are many reasons why a man may act like this. He may like a woman overly dependent upon him. He may never have felt worthwhile, and he may need to remind himself that he is, in comparison to his wife, a good person.

Case 2: Daddy's Little Helper

A mother and father have an only child, a daughter. The mother started to drink heavily as their daughter started high school. Both father and daughter feel bad that she drinks. Secretly, the daughter enjoys taking over the mother's responsibilities such as planning the meals, or keeping her father company when the mother is sick. The father enjoys being her hero and playing host to her friends. This little family triangle doesn't think the mother needs help.

Case 3: The Drinking Couple

The husband travels for business. He is a heavy drinker and a jealous man. He rationalizes, "If I control others through drink, I won't get hurt." He likes his wife to stay at home. She is much younger than he, and he worries that she may tire of him. She is safe as a lone drinker. When he comes home, he wants company when he drinks. As long as she drinks, he can control her, be mean (even violent) to her, and avoid facing his own drinking problem.

Case 4: The He-Man

The husband feels unsure of his masculinity. He feels so feminine that he fears he may be homosexual. He marries a woman who is domineering and masculine in her manner. She drinks to feel feminine and, as alcohol renders her helpless, he gains the dominant position. He plays the roles of victim, rescuer, and persecutor. He is the victim of a domineering wife. He is the rescuer by showing her how feminine she can be, and he is the persecutor by keeping her drinking.

Case 5: A Pillar In The Community

The husband has a career that puts him in the public eye. He may, for example, be a doctor, lawyer, politician, or judge. His wife may be in a public profession such as a teacher or a volunteer worker, the perfect complement for a man in a public position. His wife becomes an alcoholic. He feels her alcoholism is a dangerous reflection on his position in the community. In his eyes, alcoholism is not an illness but a mark of failure. He prefers to hide this mark of failure from the world rather than have her go into treatment. He may nag her about her drinking. His nagging makes him feel grand and independent. It may also cover an unconscious wish on his part to drink with her.

Case 6: The Hard Worker

The husband is an anxious person. He cannot show love, excitement, or joy. He is a hard worker who brings financial security to the marriage but not fulfillment. To avoid any unpleasant tension within himself when his wife is under stress, he and his wife avoid all issues by politely drinking. This becomes their means of communication. Such an uncommunicative husband needs a wife with a problem. As long as she drinks, he does not have to show emotion.

Why Women Marry Men With Problems

Psychiatrists tell us that there are many reasons why women marry men with problems. A common instance is a woman who is actively drinking, and was, because of her drinking, divorced. When she remarries (if she is still drinking), she will pick someone whom she met while drinking. He may be a heavy drinker who is extremely cruel, physically abusive, unfaithful, and shows a complete lack of concern for his marriage or family. If a woman drinks because she has problems with her feminine identity, she may pick a man who is a romeo because he may make her feel more feminine. She may pick an extremely dependent, weak man because she may be scared that any secure or strong man would leave her.

She may pick a man who likes to be dominated or hurt so that she can vent her temper. She may be angry at how her family treated her when she was a child. She has picked a husband with whom she can recreate her childhood situation to let out her recriminations, biting sarcasm, and sulkiness. When sober, she is contrite and seeks forgiveness.

A woman who had an alcoholic father may go out of her way to marry someone like him. It is her way of "keeping" her father with her. This is particularly true if the daughter blamed the mother for the father's drinking. In her own marriage she hopes that with her attitudes, which she says are different from those of her mother, she will be able to rehabilitate him. Instead, the daughter may start to drink.

A daughter may also marry a man who has the attributes of her mother. Very often, women come from homes where the mother was domineering, cold, and a perfectionist. The father was an emotionally responsive man who drank periodically. The daughter, still dependent upon her mother, lacks self-confidence and feels she is like her father. She marries a domineering man like her mother and drinks like her father.

She may have a need to have a subtly sadistic relationship with her husband in which she is demanding, whining, and petulant. She succeeds in arousing guilt in her husband to keep the relationship going. First, she'll accuse him, "You don't love me," or she'll say, "I know you are unfaithful to me." She will finally fall back on real or imagined inadequacies in herself. "If it weren't for my miserable menstrual cramps, you know I would not behave like this." Only a man with strong needs to be debased and dominated would tolerate such dialogue.

The Man Who Keeps His Wife Out of Treatment

Husbands such as those in these case histories may fill their wives' ears with all kinds of "legitimate" reasons for staying out of treatment.

He'll tell her that the children need her and "we can't afford baby sitters." She is still managing the home well. He may hint to his wife that her long absenteeism in a treatment center, halfway house, or evenings spent at AA may tempt him into the arms of another woman. He will tell her that Al-Anon is not for him.

He may humiliate her. "You're so stupid, so helpless, so ugly that if it weren't for me, you'd be in the gutter." He won't let her know what she is really worth to her family when she is sober.

He may just plain discourage her. "You don't fit in with that therapy group. You can do much better on your own. You really don't have a problem. Only weak people have a problem. You can stop drinking any time you choose to."

When such a husband closes all doors to treatment, an emergency, such as a car accident, a pass out, or a youngster in the family rebelling against society because of his or her anger about the situation at home, may cause an abrupt break in the family routine. At that point, countless agencies with the proper counselors are ready to step in.

Once the family is in treatment, it may be difficult to keep them in treatment. The husband may let his wife go into treatment because he wants to help. As she gets better, he may encourage her to leave the treatment center too early because the family "needs" her. The counselor may explain to him why his wife should continue in the center. His denial of their problems may be so strong that he cannot listen to any reason. If the husband has not been going right along to Al-Anon or family counseling, he may feel that the family equilibrium, even if it is a poor family equilibrium, may be threatened. He fears that his wife is beginning to understand what stresses and hostile dependencies there are in their marriage. He has, up to now, suffered along with the alcoholic and when she arrests her drinking, he may be getting the message that she will no longer let herself be controlled by him, and he should do something about his problems, too. The greater the denial of his anxieties, the more he will do to keep her out of treatment. An anxious person will try to protect himself against feelings of shame and guilt.

He may try to do it by "intellectualizing" instead of getting in touch with his emotions. For instance, he may say, "My wife drinks because her parents spoiled her." He should be talking about what her drinking has done to him and how he could give her support. He should be getting in touch with his own emotions.

When She Does Stop Drinking

He should know that the therapist has compassion for what he went through while his wife was drinking. While she was actively drinking, the father may have assumed the mothering chores. The children may be used to listening only to the father. When the alcoholic woman gives up drinking and resumes her mothering role, the father is faced with a rival for the affection of the children. The youngsters understandably may present behavior problems for a time and this is a strain on the whole family. In some cases, without proper counseling or AA, Al-Anon, and Alateen, the family may end up in the divorce court.

It is important to understand the feelings of the husband. Even when the husband recognizes that alcoholism is an illness, subtle gestures, such as the arrested alcoholic looking worried or depressed like she used to before she went on a binge, or using the same heavy cologne and make-up she used to put on during her drinking years, may frighten him into a stony withdrawal and old self-defenses.

Sex may be a problem, too. Some women when they become sober still have a deep feeling of unworthiness. The same feeling that drove them to drink makes them feel unworthy of their sex partners. If they had a rigid, moralistic upbringing, they may equate sex and liquor as equal evils. Such women, if they abstain from liquor, may also abstain for a while from sex. The past may haunt a husband, too.

A woman repulsed by sex may perform well when drunk. As her drinking progresses, her partner will be repulsed when she is drunk, and she, being drugged with alcohol, may not understand his repulsion. In anger, she may humiliate him. These are difficult scenes to forget, even when the alcoholic arrests her drinking. He may have a hard time finding her attractive again. Counseling for both husband and wife and much patience may change the course of this marriage.

All sexual problems become magnified with alcohol, but they don't disappear with arrested drinking. This is seen over and over again in the alcoholic marriage. It has been noticed when a couple or the spouse arrests their or her drinking, they may get a divorce. These couples, if they married while they were drinking already, may never have known what they were like sober. As counseling proceeds, they may find out that they are really incompatible. Incompatibility is not necessarily a hopeless situation. In some cases, if the couple has the patience to seek help, they may find out that they could have a future together.

While one or both parties are drinking, there are moments of hate, poor judgment, bewilderment, and anger.

THE DRINKING WOMAN: REVISITED

Al-Anon and Alcoholics Anonymous stress that it is important to look upon these problems less with a "what happened in our past" attitude and more with the "conviction that most of us have the power to bring about substantial changes in our relationship and living conditions, by searching out and correcting our own shortcomings. As such changes occur, each of us will know what course of action is right for the particular time and situation."

Many Husbands Want Healthy Wives

Not all cases are as severe as those cited in this chapter. A woman may become an alcoholic in a healthy marriage, too. Such was the case of a very dependent woman married to a traveling salesman. She was unhappy being alone night and day. She did not know how to keep herself busy. She drank to compensate for her loneliness. The husband saw her predicament and encouraged her to go to Alcoholics Anonymous. He went to Al-Anon in whatever town he was visiting. After the meeting, he always phoned his wife so that they could talk about the experiences at their respective meetings.

Here are a husband and wife who openly said, "We need each other; let's tackle this together." If the alcoholic can be made to see her problems and her husband can be made to see his problems, treatment can proceed well. If still married, the family is a woman's prime supportive source.

The more a husband and wife deny the need for each other and try to solve their problems separately, the less chance there is to keep the marriage. A husband and wife should be able to be dependent upon each other for basic satisfactions, strength, and fulfillment. An ideal relationship is one where each one feels accepted by the other, where there is a feeling of mutual protection, prestige, a sense of accomplishment, and psychological independence. A marriage should be a relationship that is not exploited by either partner and where drink is not needed to make it work.

A few years ago women would have been afraid to discuss such problems so openly. Today, at closed therapy meetings for women only and at all other treatment facilities, these problems are discussed freely.

Updates
- Heavy drinkers like to marry fellow heavy drinkers.
- Having had close childhood family bonds contributes to a successful harmonious marriage.
- In their book, *The Longevity Project*, Dr. Howard S. Friedman and Dr. Leslie R. Martin reveal on page 120 that "if you were a prudent and responsible child (such as no teenage drinking) . . . you were . . . more likely . . . to have a successful marriage." (*The Longevity Project* is based on Dr. Lewis M. Terman's studies. In 1921 he sought out 1,521 girls and boys with high I.Q. in California who were studied to the end of their lives. For our purposes it is interesting to note that some grew up to be heavy drinkers. These far reaching longitudinal studies allow the researchers to sort some of the causes and effects of problems, choice of life styles, and the resulting health and longevity.)
- Throughout the book, *The Longevity Project*, the authors point out over and over that their study showed that people can change. On page 6 they mention, "—people can change—albeit slowly and with substantial effort.—placing oneself in groups where we will meet new people—we can analyze our actions—and vigilantly monitor and correct for any slip backs—" on page 57 the authors state, "Many Terman subjects faced serious challenges—those who circled back to the healthy road often went on to a long life."
- Studying the Terman questionnaires filled out by the 1521 boys and girls who came from different emotional backgrounds Dr. Friedman and Dr. Martin noted that those who came from divorced homes did not necessarily have poor marriages or an unhealthy life style (such as drinking too much). They sum it up on page 92 "—it may make working at one's own situation particularly important with correspondingly greater benefits."
- Behavioral Couple Therapy aids couples to achieve abstinence and to improve their relationships. The outpatient therapy is geared to help an alcoholic spouse as well as

couples where both have a drinking problem. Techniques include signing contracts to refrain from drinking. The husband and wife or significant other help each other to follow her/his contract. The couples learn how to identify and alleviate stresses and to join non-alcoholic couple activities. Communication skills are as well emphasized. Partially funded by the National Institute of Health more information may be received from Timothy J. O'Farrell, Ph.D., ABPP (508)-583-4500 ext. 63493 timothyofarrell@hms.harvard.edu.

- An alcoholic who has been prescribed disulfiram to make drinking undesirable does better when a spouse observes when she takes the prescribed amount each day. If she fails to take the prescription and/or drinks he can inform the physician or therapist who can then decide how to handle the problem. It leaves the husband out of any unpleasant discussions about her drinking.
- Couples therapy permits the husband to describe what his wife's drinking has done to their marriage. It prevents the alcoholic wife from minimizing or denying her condition.
- Some family therapies such as offered by the Ackerman Institute will include the children so that they may have the opportunity to understand what has made their lives so difficult and that alcoholism runs in families. The children learn from a skilled therapist that they can avoid triggering this disease, alcoholism, in their lives.
- Wives are probably more sensitive than husbands. Dr. Friedman and Dr. Martin on page 124 of their Longevity Project (previously introduced in this chapter) affirmed after studying the questionnaires of the Terman participants that a wife's well-being is much more affected by a difficult husband than a husband's well-being is affected by a hostile wife.
- Women who are dependent on their husbands' incomes may stay in their marriages even
- if their chances of recovery are better without their husbands.

- Marriage may help a woman cope. A husband who is sober may make sure that his wife takes her medicine, call for help if his wife passes out or has a heart attack and encourage her to seek help if he notices any symptoms.
- The Terman study showed that divorce was less harmful to women's health than to men's health.
- "Enabler" is a frequently used term today to describe a spouse who ignores his wife's drinking. The Merriam Webster Dictionary defines the term as "—one who enables another to persist in self-destructive behavior (as substance abuse) by providing excuses or by making it possible to avoid the consequences of such behavior."
- Husbands and children are often tired of approaching an alcoholic wife and/or mother to stop drinking, because she may react abusively. The best time to suggest treatments such as joining Alcoholics Anonymous or private therapy is when the alcoholic wakes up sick with a hangover, immediately after an arrest for drunk driving, or after upsetting and unseemly behavior.

CHAPTER 7

FEMALE SEXUALITY AND ALCOHOLISM

Some women may drink heavily because they are afraid of their womanhood. This fear encompasses much more than pregnancy and intercourse. All women, not just alcoholics, have moments of doubt. These doubts are mostly understandable. The woman who is expecting her first baby may wonder if bodies do truly open so wide as to let a baby out. The first time a girl has intercourse, she may confuse her inexperience with insufficiency. A woman may feel insecure if she is trying to conceive and does not meet with immediate success. However, the alcoholic woman is much more sensitive to such very normal doubts because she has, to begin with, a poor image of herself and may use alcohol to bolster her feelings.

Women and Their Images

A great deal of how a woman feels about herself as a woman has to do with how her family, her culture, and her religion treats her. If she had a father who looked down on women, mistreated her mother, referred to women in unflattering terms as "broads," "never trust a woman driver," it may well make her wonder about herself. On the other hand, if she had a father who was accepting, loving, and kind, she will feel secure as a woman. If her mother had positive outlooks about her own health, her children, and her place in the family and community, she will have gathered strength from such a woman.

Sometimes a woman may dislike a mother and unconsciously choose to copy a father. Lynn explained it the following way to a group of women: "When I arrested my drinking, I was in treatment with a psychiatrist. He told me that I had admired my father so much that I copied him and consequently deviated from the normal sex role behavior. I did such things as have 'one too many' with the boys in the office after work. At first, I couldn't understand what the psychiatrist meant. After all, I did get married, I did have a baby. But the doctor meant there were many ways I could copy my father such as his drinking habits. As we inspected my life, I realized that my mother had been a perfectionist who showed little emotion or warmth. She tried to dominate all of us in the family. My father was a warm and giving person but a weak husband. Since my father was easier to get along with, even when he was intoxicated, I chose him as a model."

Sometimes a woman will copy a father because she wants to identify with the stronger adult in the family.

Dr. P., a gynecologist, tells of a sweet young woman who wanted a child very badly.

"It was important for her to have a child to prove to herself her female identity. She conceived with difficulty and always miscarried within the first twelve weeks of her pregnancy. She had a heavy drinking problem. She did have a child after going to Alcoholics Anonymous. It was years later that she told me that it took her a long time to realize that she never quite felt sure of herself as a woman. The more she worked on the problem, the more she came to understand that her father, who had been an alcoholic, brutalized her mother. She never could understand her mother putting up with all the cruelties and injustices. Self-defense made her model herself after the stronger parent. In this case, it was her father."

Women who feel uncomfortable about their sex do not make full use of their talents, earning power, mothering capabilities, or capacity for sexual enjoyment. They may be afraid of sex and concentrate their drives on romantic fantasies rather than go to bed with a man.

Drink may help them to fantasize. Such deprived women feel that they must always be gorgeous, and all their energies will go into making up their faces, doing their hairstyles and, in general, trying to look sexy.

Our parents alone do not form our outlooks. Our personal ideals of what we as women want may be in conflict with our background.

Society, religion, and culture impose many unfair taboos on women. Until recently, a girl was supposed to do no more than pet. Remember? Sweet sixteen and never been kissed!

These attitudes from a more conservative milieu still exercise a powerful influence today. Prudent girls, with all the public knowledge of sex available to them, may rebel but still feel guilty that they have "gone all the way." Some of these girls, when they reach middle-age, may feel they have not had full lives. Some feel dissatisfied without knowing why. Others are divorced or abandoned by their husbands and feel the break-ups are their fault because they are inadequate women. They think, "Who would want me?" and do not have the courage to make new lives for themselves. Some of these women find it less fearsome to sit home and drink.

A woman too often assumes that if sex isn't right it is all her fault. The woman doesn't voice her feelings about sex because she is afraid her partner might go elsewhere for his sex. If she is nervous, the vagina naturally contracts and he cannot enter her body easily. Under such circumstances, sex can then be painful for a woman. A woman may also experience pain when the man is in such a hurry that there is not enough foreplay. The vagina does not then give off the lubrication needed to make the entry of the penis easy.

Needless to say, not all women who come from conservative backgrounds have problems. Many such women enjoy their married lives and positions in the society and family. But until recently, those who needed help had nowhere to go for help. These women feel overpowered, humiliated, and inferior in their marriages. Under these circumstances, it is quite likely that the woman may feel incapable of reaching an orgasm. One woman in a treatment center said she drank because her husband had left her. He felt she was frigid. She summed it up by calling it "legalized rape." Another patient answered her, "Instead of drinking after your husband left you, you should have taken a few stiff drinks before you had sex with him."

In the past, most women who lived in such a marriage felt that there was something wrong with them. Sometimes they had the courage to confide their problems to a gynecologist. Since the gynecologist usually was a man, his advice was all too apt to be a logical extension of his own outlook because, at that time, little was known about a woman's orgasm and needs. The doctor usually counseled, "Make things romantic. Have dinner by candle light. Have a few cocktails first." It never occurred to the good doctor that he was encouraging the use of alcohol as a coping mechanism by a woman who might be predisposed to alcoholism.

Dramatic changes have taken place in the last 15 years. Doctors are making it their business to communicate better with their patients. The National Organization of Women sponsors all day health sessions in many cities. Many Y's open their doors to organized lectures and rap sessions. There are now over 150 self-help gynecology clinics throughout the U.S.A.

Doctors do not know as much as they would like to about women. Gynecologists are still trying to understand the aspects of a woman's orgasm. They know that a little alcohol (no more than one or two cocktails) may take the edge off an inhibited woman and help her to have an orgasm, but too much alcohol may keep any woman from having an orgasm.

Coping With Gynecological Problems

Most healthy women adjust one way or another to unexpected problems. For instance, a non-alcoholic woman who had problems conceiving or who miscarries easily might go to a gynecologist for a checkup. Her husband might be asked to go for a sperm count. Whether medical care is needed or not, they might decide to adopt a child, and perhaps later, they will have a child of their own. Or, the wife may decide to work until she does become pregnant. If the woman feels that she may be having problems because her background gave her a disturbed sex-role identity, she might decide to go into counseling or to participate in a consciousness-raising group or to attend courses which discuss the subject. These are all healthy ways in which to deal with life.

An alcoholic woman will drink, and therefore, magnify her situation into a more severe problem. If she drinks, her gynecologist won't know what is caused by the drinking and what is caused by physical or psychological problems.

Gynecologists note that such difficulties as inability to conceive or miscarrying easily occur more frequently in the alcoholic woman than in a healthy woman. Her alcoholic way of life, which includes the physical effects of alcohol on her body, will cause trouble. She may fall easily and cause a miscarriage. Her sleep, so vital to women trying to carry out a pregnancy, may be disturbed by the alcohol in her system. Her diet may be so poor as to affect her menstrual cycle. Chronic alcoholism may cause liver damage which could result in menstrual irregularities. Before such a woman can be helped, she has to stop drinking.

In order for a woman to understand herself, she must also understand her biological being. In many instances, what we learn from outside sources about menstruation (and other aspects of our sexual being) may be in conflict with what we learn at home. One woman at a consciousness-raising group said, "When I was in puberty, our school taught sex education. But when I was a child, I used to hear women talk at home in a warning and ominous whisper about the "curse," how one should not ride a bicycle or go to gym when one has her period. We were told in our family that it is perfectly natural to have cramps and that we should even expect to have cramps." Such a woman may have cramps to a greater degree than if she had been told that menstruation is not a "curse" but a normal female function. Such woman may receive medicine for cramps when actually they should be opening up their feelings to a sympathetic listener about how scary, mysterious and embarrassing her "curse" was the first time.

It is not uncommon for young girls who don't know too much about their bodies to get upset when they have a mild cramp, and thereby intensify it into pain. Such a girl may tend to go to bed with a hot water bottle when an examination by a gynecologist might reveal that all she needs is more exercise throughout the month, a proper diet and enough sleep. Of course, in a few cases, some may need medical care. One girl in a treatment center said that from the time she was twelve years old her mother used to give her tea with brandy for her cramps. This author herself remembers when drinking in women's college dormitories was forbidden. Tonics for "the monthlies" were permitted even though a whiff of these tonics was enough to leave no doubt in the housemother's mind as to their contents.

Any woman who is confused about her identity and has doubts about her feminine worth will feel doubly threatened by anything like premenstrual cramps, miscarriage, infertility and, finally, menopause. These women may actually "wait" for the symptoms of premenstrual cramps or menopausal discomfort and magnify them. An operation on the uterus or ovaries or an abortion will upset these women more than it would the woman who feels positive about her feminine worth. The death of a husband, parent, or child, or a desertion by the husband, divorce, or marital troubles are too much for her to bear. She will also be upset by the demands of small children. Such women, whether they drink or not, may run to doctors to complain about normal female functions. They are thus in danger of receiving too much medicine such as tranquilizers, pain killers, or sleeping pills. All women, even well-adjusted women, receive more medication in their lifetime than men.

Just as in the old days when we gave some women too many opiates and too much alcohol because doctors felt helpless whenever women complained, so today do we give her too many pills. We have pills for menstrual cramps, pills to detain menstruation, pills to bring on a period, pills to control birth, pills to abort pregnancy (morning-after pills), injections to help her to hold her pregnancy, medicine to help her in labor, medicine to induce labor (sometimes for the doctor's convenience), pills to help her counteract water retention, pills to keep her estrogen level up during menopause, and pills for her nerves. Brecher (1972) reports that in 1967 over 60% of all barbiturates, non-barbituate sedative-hypnotics, anti-anxiety agents, psychoactive drugs, anti-depressants, and amphetamines prescribed were for women. Any woman who is predisposed to alcoholism is in danger of misusing her medication, especially any mood-altering drug. Such women may take too much of the medicine, and may well take it in conjunction with alcohol.

Biology Is Destiny

A woman's life has certain tension areas that men don't have to face. We know that men have to face tensions, too, but someone else will have to write a book about theirs.

These special tension areas with which a woman has to deal do not automatically make a woman into an alcoholic, but she may seize upon anyone of them or all of them as cause for drinking.

Divorce

One of the very common problems today is divorce. According to the National Center for Health Statistics, at least four out of ten marriages end in divorce. In most cases, women want to keep the children. This means that she has to face the children's anger that the family broke up.

If the husband was unfaithful, she may feel the children are too young to be told, and the children, unknowingly, may blame her for the break-up. She cannot as easily and as quickly seek a new partner as can her ex-husband. She has to spend more time with the children as well as concern herself about finding the proper sitters for them. Often when the children are young, she cannot afford sitters and, therefore, may not even be able to get out to be with other adults.

If one of the reasons for the divorce was because she drank, it is exceedingly important that she and the children seek immediate help. A divorce sometimes jars a woman into doing something about her drinking. Now that her husband is gone, she realizes she can't afford to drink. The children need her. Once her husband is gone, the cause for her drinking may have disappeared with him. She may have drunk because he was too authoritarian, or a very cold person, or absent too much from the home. The reverse is true, too. Some women who never drank may do so after a divorce because they are lonely and frightened by their new responsibilities.

Contraception

Another area where a woman suffers more than a man is in birth control. There are some good birth control methods to use. But they are not perfectly effective, they are not always available, and they tend to put the burden of choice, acquisition, use, maintenance, and risk on the woman instead of on the man and woman together. If the woman takes the pill, she may well be concerned about its effects on a long-term basis. Will it someday cause her to have a heart attack? Do we know all the side-effects of the pill? If she drinks, she may forget to take the pill. If she manages to remember to take the pill, she must realize that both the pill and alcohol are metabolized in the liver. We don't know how the combination affects a woman's liver.

Some women feel self-conscious about using birth control methods. Many churches, schools, and families have anti-sex attitudes and, unknowingly, may make women feel self-conscious. Such women may end up with misleading or inadequate information about birth control. If a woman is inexperienced and away from home, she may not know where to get information. Birth control is a burden for the inexperienced girl. She may be shy about going to Planned Parenthood to get information. She may be afraid to seek a private doctor. If she is poor and doesn't know where to get free supplies, she may pay for the supplies at great sacrifice. Frequently, a man will refuse to wear a condom even if it is necessary for only one time. He may tell her that condoms keep him from feeling the intercourse. If she has had too much to drink, she may not know that he is penetrating her. As a result, she may be prey to venereal disease and in danger of becoming pregnant. If she gets pregnant, it is her fault.

Abortion

An unwanted pregnancy can mean heartbreak. The woman may have no means of support except welfare, or may have to choose to give up the child for adoption. Abortion is a difficult choice and may leave scars. Some women are confused about abortions even if they are for abortion. Just because a woman herself chooses to have an abortion does not mean she does not feel mournful and, in some cases, like a murderess. She may have been brought up thinking that it is wrong to have an abortion and that it is wrong to have sex out of wedlock. Since abortions are not mourned or talked about as any other death would be, the pain is internalized and may underline the stress, doubts, and hurt that are already part of her life. A woman who does not face the pain of loss may find that it may bother her later on in life when she may least expect it. Treatment centers catering to alcoholics have on occasion found that a woman will say, "I started to drink only after my abortion."

The Reason For Having Children

Some women may choose to have children. Ideally, children should be wanted for all the right reasons. The right reason would be the desire to love and to care for a child. Some women, unfortunately, have had children to prove their femininity. Others, because their families expected it of them. Here are some comments made by women in treatment centers who are alcoholic mothers:

> "I wanted a child to give it a better life than I had."
> "I knew I was going to flunk out of college anyway so I got married and had a child instead."
> "My husband had a girl friend, and I thought I could save our marriage."
> "I needed love. It was only after the baby was born that I realized the baby couldn't give me the love I needed."
> "I hated working so I found a man who could support me. My present to him was an heir.
> I didn't know that household and child care would involve such isolation and loneliness."

Pregnancy

Pregnancy forces a woman to deal with changes in her body. Some of these changes may make her happy such as the feeling of life in her body. Other changes, such as losing her figure temporarily, may make her sad. Some women rightly feel sexy when they are pregnant. An active alcoholic might use alcohol to deal with any of the discomforts of pregnancy, such as a constant feeling of tiredness, some edema (swelling), and fear of labor. Here are some statements about pregnancy taken from an all-women's therapy group.

> "I hated my figure, and then I got a phone call that my husband was having an affair. He denied it. I never felt the same about myself, the baby, or my marriage."

"Pregnancy reminded me of my youth. It reminded me of the birth of my younger brother who was always preferred. I was frequently angry during my pregnancy and hoped I would have a girl."

"I hated pregnancy because it made me feel tied down to an unhappy marriage. I had to give up my work, and I didn't want to be dependent on my husband."

"I gave up drinking during pregnancy. I wanted a child badly. Someone of my own to hold and to love. It was only after the child was born that I resumed drinking."

Baby Blues

After a child is born, a mother may have what is known as baby blues or postpartum emotional problems. Normally, these mood swings are temporary. The mother may feel the separation from the infant after having carried the child for nine months. The mother may have been the center of attention until the child was born. Many feel tied down and cannot believe that this will ever change. Some can't fall asleep again after the night feedings. "I used to say to myself my life will never be the same again. Once you are a mother, there is no going back."

These are all very normal feelings. Most families adjust and are happy that their family is growing. For most women, child-bearing is a joyful occasion and no cause for her to be depressed.

For some parents, though, the postpartum period may bring clashes of child care ideas and conflicting ideas of religious upbringing and financial strain. If the family has other children, the mother may, in addition, be overworked. Some mothers use alcohol in the hope that it will relieve them from these stresses.

Menopause

Another occasion women list as a "reason" for starting to drink is their menopausal years. Women hear so many things about menopause. Some women's monthly periods simply taper off or become irregular until menopause has been completed. Others have heard about uncomfortable symptoms such as sudden hot flashes, extreme chills or shivers, heavy bleeding, and the possibility of ovarian tumors.

Some fear the possibility of surgery for a hysterectomy. These are only some possible menopausal symptoms, and no woman will ever experience all of them. Probably most women, except for the cessation of menstruation, have no symptoms. If a woman is in need of sympathy and attention, she may hang on to every little twinge she feels to get that attention. Some women do not get enough consideration from their families at this important time of their lives. These mothers have, up to now, given a lot of themselves to the family, and it is now time for the family to give her some attention.

Menopause is often the time of life when a woman's children leave the nest; it may be the time when her husband is at the peak of his career, and he has no time for her. If she has never had confidence in herself as a woman, she may think this is the time he will seek out another woman. Since our culture does idealize youth and sex, a sensitive, insecure menopausal woman may take this aspect of our society too seriously.

If she is single and very close to her parents, it may be the time old age or death besets them, and she feels suddenly abandoned. Whether married or single, an insecure woman will consider the whole menopausal experience a personal loss. An alcoholic woman will use all these emotions as a rationalization to drink. Many women who never drank before may start to drink to help overcome depression.

Menopause is accompanied by a hormonal change which may include a lowered estrogen level. Some gynecologists feel that a deficiency in the hormone estrogen can cause nervousness, irritability, and depression, and prescribe estrogen to women in menopause. Lately, gynecologists have begun to question whether the administering of estrogen to women to help them during menopause may not in part cause them to develop uterine cancer.

The interrelation of our hormonal change and our physical and mental well-being is very complex.

Women who sit home and wait for menopausal symptoms, who think continually what medicine they'll have to take during menopause, and if they take the medicine, what it can do to them, can make themselves ill. Feeling discouraged, they may drink too much, and not eat properly or exercise insufficiently, all vital to a woman's well-being.

If a woman used her female functions to have the children she wanted, menopause should not cause her psychological problems. Unfortunately, too many women see themselves only as mothers and sex objects. Menopause makes them feel they have reached a dead-end road. It is also a time of life when we take inventory of ourselves.

Single women may feel they did not get as far in their careers as they had wanted to because they spent too much time nursing old parents. They may also, feel they did not spend as much time having fun because they were tied down to their parents or had unfair moral values, imposed upon them by their culture.

Married women may have other dissatisfactions. They may feel the children did not reach the goal they wanted for them and blame themselves. Maybe their marriages were never what they had expected, and they may regret not having had the courage to get out and seek a new partner. Perhaps their sex life with their husband was not as good or as frequent as they had wanted it, and now they feel cheated.

In reality, women have a second chance in life after menopause. They can have sex without worry of pregnancy. Since the children no longer need them, they are free to pursue their favorite sports, careers, or hobbies. One woman who started to drink during menopause and was put into treatment said, "There is nothing I know how to do except to take care of a house. I know I could work as a housekeeper, but I don't want to work for another family." After gaining more insight into her problems she started to work in a catering business. She helped charities, businesses, and families organize and budget their parties. Having a creative flair, she was paid extra to arrange the centerpieces for the tables. She had taken all these capabilities of hers for granted. It got so that her husband complained that she was so busy that he didn't get enough time to spend with her.

Two Difficult Problems

For each woman, life has brought different experiences. Each one of us has different strengths and weaknesses. So much for hard core. facts. So much for what doctors say. What matters is what has happened to each one of us and, what it has done to us. Let us listen to and learn from some of the sex problems women have discussed in treatment centers. Some stories may shock, some may seem like extreme cases, but they deserve to be aired.

Incest

One of the most difficult subjects for a woman to talk about is incest. She may have been sexually abused, in any of several ways, by an uncle, a drunken father or a stepfather. She may blame herself for not having been able to cope with the relative who abused her. Many families take the position that a girl is automatically a temptress, the local Eve in the Garden of Eden, and therefore, she brings all sexual abuses upon herself.

Such women must get past the stage of assuming all the guilt. Unfortunately, it takes women years to get up the courage to talk about their incestuous experiences. She must be convinced by the helping profession that her experience is not unique, that she is still intact, and that many women who are not alcoholics have gone through the same experience, some at an age as young as eight or nine. Diane K. told the following story:

Diane K.
"When I was ten years old, my mother took a job in the evening as a waitress. We needed the money because my father drank, and he was never able to hold a job. When she went out to work, my father baby-sat for me. Sometimes he took me to the movies. In the movies, he would always put his hand on my thighs. He called it a father's special love. When my mother went out in the evening, he would drink heavily, and it was only when he drank heavily that he would lie beside me on my bed because he said he was lonely. He was, he would remind me, my father. He would caress me, kiss me, and press his penis against me. He was usually too drunk to penetrate me. I found him repulsive. He smelled of alcohol. I was angry that my mother let me get into such a situation. It also confused me. I didn't know if my father was different from other fathers. Was I a bad daughter because I did not like what he did?

"When my mother divorced my father and remarried four years later, most of my friends had started to date. I stayed to myself. When I did go out, I felt comfortable only when I drank. The school authorities one day discovered me passed out in the girls' bathroom. My mother's second husband insisted that I be put in treatment with a psychiatrist. I would never have had the courage to tell anyone about my father, but the psychiatrist asked me point blank where I learned to drink. When I told him the first drunk I knew was my father who drank while my mother worked at night, he asked me what this drinking father did with me when we were alone."

Diane K. was lucky that she received help at a young age. Some women live with this secret for years. We have to expect some sort of damage as a result of these experiences. In their hurt, some women may become promiscuous. Others may become afraid of sex. Frequently, such women may seek out passive men who won't mind confused and frigid partners. An extreme case is Susan.

Susan, the Bar Fly
"I used to be called Susan, the bar fly; Susan, from Skid Row; and Susan, the prostitute. None of these names is very nice, but then, neither was my life. Oddly enough, no one ever called me Susan, the alcoholic. That is what I should have been called—just Susan, the alcoholic.

"I was confused, lonely and frigid. I used to seek companionship in bars. My drunkenness made people think that I was a loose woman. In our society, drunkenness and women conjure up in people's minds thoughts of the bar fly. It never occurs to people that we may be seeking nothing more than companionship, shelter, and money for drink.

"My story is long and ugly. I never knew my father. He ran out on us after I was born. My older sister remembers him vaguely. She said that he drank a lot. I always felt my mother blamed my birth as the reason for my father's walking out on us. My mother seemed mostly angry and hostile to me. She slapped me frequently. My mother preferred my sister. She never slapped her as much and never gave her as many household chores. When I had a problem, I didn't dare go to my sister because she would tell my mother, and my mother would slap me.

"One day a man moved in with us. I called him Uncle Charles. He drank a lot. I was 14 at the time. One hot summer day, I wore shorts around the apartment. I was lying on the floor watching television. Charles came out of the bedroom and raped me. As he completed the act, my mother walked in. She threw Charles out. She also called me a slut for lying around in shorts. I never forgave her for that.

"My only solace was the church. I told our nun a little about my life. I didn't dare tell her everything. I began to daydream about my real father, whom I had never known. In my fantasies, he loved me. He was terrific. I drank like him, too. Then I stopped going to church because I was ashamed to go to church drunk. My own family threw me out. I knew I could make a quick buck in the street. I would do anything for a fix, a drink, or both."

Such cases make some of us cry out in pain. But such women can be helped if they want to be helped and if they get the right counselor in the helping profession.

First of all, a woman like Susan has to be made to feel worthwhile. Because of how her mother treated her, a woman like Susan may have gotten the idea that she's inadequate as a human being. Her experience with her Uncle Charles may have caused her to be repulsed by men.

Susan isn't alone. Many alcoholic women talk about having had sex at a too young age—12, 13, 14. Frequently, the first sex act was forced on her and unpleasant. Many people try to sweep these facts under the rug. And yet the facts can haunt us. Years later, we may still not relax. We may be more interested in receiving sex than participating in sex. We will try to enjoy sex, but, because of our poor experiences, we are not equipped to participate wholeheartedly.

When Susan was in treatment, she talked about how, "I never really had orgasms. Sometimes I had incomplete orgasms. I considered myself frigid for all the wrong reasons and drink sure helped. Alcohol became my most intimate and desired experience. Anything else, including sex, was inconsequential. I learned a lot about myself in treatment. I came to realize that I blamed myself for what happened with my mother's boy friend. Deep down, I thought it was my fault. I felt so guilty that I let any one in this world punish me by abusing me. I purposely picked rejecting men so that I could be a victim. If people were mean to me, it calmed my guilt feelings. I literally let men rape me because I felt that this was all I was worth. My doctor told me that when I am raped, I can convince myself that I am not promiscuous because rape cannot be my fault. My doctor also tells me that I may have masculine strivings because I hated my mother. I identified with my imaginary father."

Not every woman in Susan's position is as determined to understand her life and to straighten it out.

Sapphism

Another subject which deserves discussion and which treatment centers say they wish they knew more about is the correlation between alcoholism and lesbianism. At this point, we can only make generalizations about alcoholics and lesbians. Counselors specializing in alcoholism claim more and more female homosexuals are surfacing. Some of these women go to homosexual bars to seek out partners. These bars promote drinking.

Case History: Marcia

Marcia is one such case. She tells: "I lost my mother at a very young age. My father kept saying, 'I wish you were a boy.' To please him, I dressed in unfeminine clothes. My father did not pay much attention to me. He was cold and aloof. I noticed that I was not developing as much as the other girls. I was comparatively flat-chested. I didn't get my period until I was 16. My father had a sister who had never married and lived with another woman. I felt very comfortable and accepted there. When I was with other girls and boys, I felt I was awkward and unfeminine. When I went away to college, there was a bar nearby known to attract the 'gays.' I enjoyed drinking there. It was there that

I met a girl with lots of experience. She showed me that two women staying together can be a deeply satisfying experience. Today I am an alcoholic. The treatment center I am in is trying to help me sort out my life. I think I will be a lesbian all my life, but I will be one who is an arrested alcoholic. I am learning to respect myself."

The Importance of Sharing Insights and Fears

Women who get together to talk about sex and alcoholism learn to have great tolerance for all kinds of people. Women who don't drink sometimes have the same sexual problems, but since the issue is never forced out by alcoholism, they live silently with their difficulties.

Consider the case of Carol H. What she tells us is a very common emotion among all women, although Carol used alcohol to deal with it.

"I drank when I had my menopause. The children had left home, my husband traveled a lot, and I found myself getting up in the morning for nothing. I didn't even make my bed because I knew if I did that there would be nothing for me to do after that. I knew no widowed or divorced women who could go to a movie with me. Our married friends were busy. There was no one to reassure me that I was a worthwhile, needed human being. I used to get that feeling from the children when they needed me. My husband still felt needed by his business. I felt like a discarded dish rag. I ached because of the void. I had to discover a behavior to fill that void. That behavior for me was drinking."

Women owe it to themselves to discuss these problems openly and freely. As they talk, they become liberated. As they become liberated, their consciousness is raised. When their consciousness is raised, they seek better lifestyles. We always think our own problem is the worst. As we open up our hearts, we'll find this isn't so. As women talk together they will discover no problem is truly unique. By sharing their problems they may help another woman to talk about her own deepest fears and needs.

Updates
- Dr. Janet A. Sobczak, a nurse practitioner, who has studied drug dependent women, points out that "The perception that a woman is more sexually available when she is

drinking alcohol not only contributes to the stigmatization of women, but increases the risk for violent victimization in situations involving alcohol abuse."

- Women's complaints about intercourse hurting, difficulty with orgasm and arousal ("I can only have intercourse if I drink.") are all labeled as sexual dysfunctions that can and should be treated. Dr.Sobczak after studying several research papers on the subject reports that over 40% of women are thought to have at least one sexual dysfunction. It must be remembered that other health factors than alcohol abuse, such as diabetes, coronary heart disease, may also influence these statistics. However childhood sexual abuse was found to be a persistent theme among women "who needed to drink before sex." In one specific test women with a history of sexual abuse became more aroused when given alcohol versus a placebo while the opposite was true for women with no history of sexual abuse. Women who feel also that sex is sinful and feel guilty when having sex will drink hoping to quell such distress.
- In a scientific survey it was shown that sexual desire improved significantly after a year among women who had arrested their drinking.
- Women who believe the myth that alcohol increases sexual desire are likely to report that they do feel sexual aroused after drinking. In a study (Wilson & Lawson, 1976) where arousal was objectively measured after being exposed to erotic stimuli, the results showed that women who drank measured less sexual arousal than those who did not drink.
- Homosexuality is seen today as a normal variation of human sexuality.
- Dr. Robert P. Cabaj (page 623, *The American Psychiatric Publishing Textbook of Substance Abuse Treatment 4th edition 2008*) explains that "—Lesbians (the groups most studied) have higher rates of alcohol use than the general population, have higher rates of mood and anxiety disorders—".
- Lesbians are included today more frequently in sexual studies than previously.

- Lesbians tend to gather in bars known for welcoming them.
- According to Alcoholics Anonymous, even though AA is open to everyone, some groups are limited to "designated sexual orientation," in other words known to consist mostly of lesbians.
- Larger cities have alcohol free coffee houses, bookstores and clubs catering to a lesbian clientele.
- Some lesbians use alcohol to internalize their fear of a homophobic family, colleagues, and to drown the thought of coming out. (See Chapter 13, Seeking Help, in this book)
- Lesbians who lack self-acceptance tend to encase themselves in a social group that uses alcohol to cope.

CHAPTER 8

FEMINISM

Because there are those who say that the increase in female drinking is due to the new feminism, it is important to look at our society's new open lifestyles in greater depth. In particular we shall ask how many of our new lifestyles are really no more than social conveniences and how many are within the framework of feminism. What we mean by feminism in this chapter is the same feminism as defined by our more progressive and successful helping agencies. In essence the helping agencies are saying:

> Feminism is the right to be a whole woman. Everyone should be able to test her/his qualities without having to label them male or female.

Both men and women who do not feel secure with women's new freedom say while women's liberation may release women from certain stultifying pressures, it may in turn create new and difficult choices. For example, the opening of executive jobs to women requires such things as working overtime and involves hard core selling or extensive traveling and decision-making. From these pressures women certainly cannot claim to be more immune than men.

Her new lifestyle, whatever it is, may force a woman to question her role as a woman. Has the sexual revolution, the choice of not having children, or putting children in day care centers put too many demands on women's emotions? Are all these new roles causing more women to drink?

Women Are Drinking More

It is well to approach the subject of the amount of drinking done by women today with a certain caution. To some extent, the problem has always existed. The keeping of statistics on the subject of alcoholism is relatively recent. And it is certainly true that the woman today is less reticent about coming forward and saying, "Look, I have a problem." Still, there can be little doubt that female drinking is increasing in the United States. Prior to the mid-1970s, such studies as Glatt (in 1961), Lisansky (in 1957), Schuckit (in 1972), and Wanberg and Knapp (in 1970) all reported that the onset of drinking began at a later age for women than for men, but that women lose control of their drinking faster than men.

Other studies showed that women tended to drink alone at home and hide their drinking while men frequent public places and drink in the company of other men. (Jacob and Camil, 1971 and Lisansky, 1957). In 1965, Johnson pointed out that women are more evasive about their drinking and tend to minimize their consumption.

While these studies may still reflect the situation accurately for many present-day women alcoholics, there are indications that the woman's new lifestyle is changing her drinking habits. The liberated lifestyle has placed women in drinking situations they were never expected to deal with before. More women are working outside the home. Single women do not continue to stay with their families but live alone. Because of the high divorce rate, more women are heads of families. More women are aiming for jobs traditionally held by men (construction workers, executives, etc.). This new woman may choose to copy the habits of the men she works with. That means she may decide to have a drink before she goes home, and she may already have had one at lunch. The single, woman no longer hesitates to go in a bar to make social contacts. And there are indications that she starts to drink at a younger age than did her mother. Hanson reported in 1974 that 73% of the women in college he questioned drank socially.

In a Boston study of 1,750 junior and senior high school students in middle-class and industrial neighborhoods, 88% of the girls said they were drunk on beer five times and 27% on liquor in a one-year period. This is in startling contrast to the situation among the boys, 47% of whom reported being drunk on beer at least five times in a one-year period, while 23% said they were drunk on distilled liquor. On the basis of this study, at least, the idea that young ladies drink less than boys no longer fits the facts.

Many young people, boys and girls, drink heavily to experiment, to show that they are "smart" or "grown up." Girls may especially drink to be "glamorous," "sexy," or a "good sport." A few may drink to block out sexual confusion or feelings of inferiority and cross the line from carefree social drinking to alcoholism.

Alcohol and the Working Woman

Now that we know that girls drink at a younger age, let us look at what happens to them when they start to work. To understand the working woman and drink, we have to first look very briefly at her history.

The Poor Working Girl

In the lower socio-economic group, until public assistance was introduced, women had to work.

Alcohol was sometimes the only relief poor women had from work that was often grueling, under-paid, and boring. Alcohol helped in their attempt to forget their crowded quarters, dreary lives, limited diet and aches and pains from over-work. Today, the way our welfare system is set up, a poor woman may be forced to stay home, sometimes with as many as five or seven children. The father(s) may be absent, unknown. Or, he may be hiding so that she can receive public assistance. Her problems concerning women's lib are entirely different from those of the middle-class. We will deal with poverty and its unique problems in the next chapter. We will see that some may be afraid to drink because the social worker may take her children away. Some may be afraid to take a job because she may not be able to earn as much as her social assistance pays. Consequently, a shift has taken place as to who "wants" to work. Today, it is most frequently the wife of the higher income husband who seeks work.

Middle-Class Working Women

Naturally, middle-class women work by choice to fulfill themselves and to afford more luxuries. It is safe to hazard a guess that most middle-class working ladies who are alcoholics would drink even if they had stayed home. On occasion, a middle-class alcoholic woman may be forced to work because she is divorced, widowed, or had never married and her parents have passed away. These circumstances in themselves (death of parents, a husband, and divorce), whether she works or not, may make the woman who is predisposed to alcoholism into an alcoholic.

The Career Woman

According to the latest Alcoholics Anonymous survey:

40% of their women members were housewives
20% sales clerical
20% executive, professional, and in technical fields
10% service or semi-skilled
10% other jobs

Looking at these statistics, the professional woman might say, "There—40% of the female alcoholics questioned are housewives and only 20% are executive professional women. That's twice as many housewives drinking as women executives." On the other hand, a husband who doesn't want his wife to work may add up the statistics of all the working women and say 60% of the working women are alcoholics. The professional in the field of alcoholism might say the statistics prove that women in all walks of life may become alcoholics.

What are career-minded, middle-class women alcoholics like? Personnel directors of large corporations are saying, "We are beginning to recognize the middle-class female alcoholic in our midst. Like all alcoholics, she is frequently absent from work. Her excuses for being absent are comparable to the men's. Her excuses may be, 'My mother is sick' or 'I have a virus.' When at work, she'll make frequent trips to the toilet to drink. She acts overly feminine but looks untidy. Her work is at times brilliant but inconsistent, and she is an artist at procrastinating. She won't lunch with the other women so that she can drink privately. Or, if she does eat with the other women, she doesn't drink in front of them.

Some women may feel that they have to drink along with the men in order to prove that they have made it in a man's world.

This may be true in a few cases. As a rule, though, the female manager, secretary or clerk, if she has a drinking problem, still resorts to private drinking because she feels a drunk woman is less acceptable in society than a man "who had a few too many."

Special Dynamics of the Working Woman

In many ways, the employed female alcoholic does not differ so much from the employed male alcoholic. It is part of the alcoholic pattern to work at a job below one's capacity and education. The reason alcoholics will choose an inferior job is that the less responsibility active alcoholics have, the less chance they will have of being fired. The alcohol in their system also impairs their efficiency and talent. A fulfilling job may frighten them because if they have to work at full capacity, it leaves them little time to drink.

Role Playing

There is a subtle problem affecting all working women and compounding the problem for the very sensitive alcoholic woman. Society, without realizing it, may make life more difficult for the talented woman or the woman who wants to work than for a man. What may bother a talented woman is that she does not carry out what society expects of her, such as having children, and thus, she has ambivalent feelings about her worth.

Women value their femininity and want to feel like women but not in terms of being half a human being. The role playing within a family can be confusing, not only for the mother, but also for the children. An over-simplified but valid example is that of a mother who earns more than the father, but the act that "Daddy earns more than Mommy" is still played out before the children, or worse, the act that it is wrong for "Mommy to earn more than Daddy" is implied.

Dependency Needs

If we are to look at female alcoholism honestly we must recognize that a woman may have unresolved dependency needs whether she lives under the new feminism umbrella or practices the old lifestyle. But it will be more difficult for an alcoholic woman to work out her dependency needs than it is for her male partner if she is encouraged to act continually docile and to repress her desire to grow up.

A man can and may have as many dependency needs as a woman. Dependencies are a repressed and unresolved craving for maternal care. If the mother was "cold" to the young child, if the baby was not "fed" and given affection as needed, or if the parents were at one moment warm and out-going and the next withdrawn, such experiences can leave a man as well as a woman craving for maternal love. If an adult still has these needs, there is an unresolved problem within that person.

Since in our society a man cannot show such emotions, he may instead have a temper fit every time something goes wrong, or he may choose to be a heavy smoker, or he may want his wife to baby him. A woman might show her dependency needs by crying or acting helpless. In many cases whether at home or on the job, a woman as well as a man may use alcohol to cope with dependency needs. Such a woman will use alcohol as easily when her teenage son tells her to mind her own business as when her boss tells her she did not get the promotion. An alcoholic woman (as well as a man) will always find a reason to drink. A woman will say, "The people on the job don't like me." "My husband doesn't love me." "Only the men get the good jobs."

Women sometimes suffer more from dependency needs than men because their mothers never valued or had faith in them in the same sense that they valued or had faith in their sons.

These mothers are in part like this because they look down on themselves. The dependency may be made worse by the ambivalence in the household. The ambivalence is especially bad because we preach "equal rights" for men and women but imply in our actions that women are to be treated differently. This is very confusing for a woman and damaging to her identity.

For example, a girl is told she has as much sexual freedom as a man. Yet, mothers imply to their daughters that a daughter has more rules to follow than a son, and if she does not follow these rules, she stands out more and is called "queer." A man is supposed to sow his wild oats. A girl, if she does, is supposed to do it discreetly. The contradictions are in education, too. A girl who had the opportunity to finish her education, but who didn't, looks down on herself. A man says proudly, "So what! I went through the school of hard knocks."

Unmarried girls in many families are asked to contribute to their brother's education. After all, it is reasoned, a girl can always get married. Such treatment in itself may not cause a woman to drink but it can contribute to her feelings of ambivalence about her identity, which in turn may intensify her drinking problem.

Many women were taught by their mothers that no matter how talented they are, they should use their careers only to support their husbands' educations, and if they continue to work while their husbands work, not to get more pay than their husbands.

Case History of a Drinking Career Woman

To portray the common ambivalence with which women are raised, to portray the phoniness in our society which compounds a woman alcoholic's problems, let us listen to a woman who is a M.D. and an arrested alcoholic. She told her therapy group how her family by their actions implied that her place is in the home serving the men even if she has to suppress a talent. For many of us, the story has an all too familiar ring.

"I came from a large family. My mother died when I was ten years old. I was the oldest in the family and had all the responsibilities. I was brilliant in school and my father always made fun of me because he said I should stick to 'women's work.' When I was about twelve years old, my father remarried. My stepmother was not bad to me, but I did not feel close to her. I spent a lot of time on my schoolwork and in a sense retreated within myself. My schoolwork was my greatest love. There was a subtle prejudice at home. Boys did 'boys' activities and girls did 'girls' activities. My father used to take the boys fishing but not the girls. The boys' cursing was tolerated, but we girls had to be sweet, kind, and polite. It was all right to cry. When I entered medical school, I was to learn that as differently as a girl was treated at home, as differently will be her anxiety, her abuses, and her behavior in her career.

"In medical school, I was very self-conscious to be among all these male students. Deep down, I remembered when I was a kid, my science teacher told me medical schools wanted to accept women. But when I went into a toy store, I saw girls' nurses kits and boys' medical kits. The majority of chemistry sets show only boys on the cover. What's the sense of encouraging a girl to go into a career if we don't let her feel comfortable as a child playing doctor? I needed relief from this feeling of really not belonging in a man's world. I began drinking secretly because drinking was another thing a girl was not supposed to do. I made sure though that I drank Scotch because Scotch (so the ads tell us) means acceptance and success, and I was going to be a success. All through medical school, the boys verified all I had felt at home. After a tough operation, the doctors would say, 'Let's get a drink.' This rarely included me; and when it did, I felt I had to drink like a man because it meant equal rights.

"The male medical students were less concerned with my medical ability and more with the threat I represented. 'Are you married?' they'd ask. If I said, 'Yes,' I could feel I was less of a threat. If I said 'No,' there was always the suggestion that I was looking more for a doctor husband than an education. I truly felt each vital part of my talent, my brains, my knowledge being rejected. Whenever I showed the slightest amount of leadership, I was labeled as 'masculine.'"

Are these new pressures, or are they merely pressures which women have up to now circumvented by staying out of male careers?

It is only when a woman learns to have faith in herself that she is truly independent. These spiritually independent women say that too often there have been subtle pressure, persuasion and restraint hidden in that real or fantasized masculine protection.

In a Mobile Society the Woman Is the Victim

Giving in to the psychology of our time, we find it easy to focus our attention on a highly visible but small minority of well-to-do liberated women who travel on their own and do what they please on their trips. It is closer to the truth to be reminded that married women and children are victims of the whole new mobile lifestyle imposed upon them by traveling male executives. According to American Express, recent statistics show that 21,923,000 people travel on business abroad and domestically. These statistics, based primarily on plane and ship travel, do not include businessmen who go away by car for days at a time. We can then safely assume the statistic to be higher than that mentioned here.

Some women cope very well under these circumstances. Some busy themselves with their children, make friends through volunteer work, and, if they live far from home, encourage their relatives to come for lengthy visits. Some build up careers of their own which they "pack up" and continue when their husbands are transferred.

Others have a hard time. They can't make new friends because they are shy. Their families can't come and visit because they are tied down themselves or can't afford it. Still other women who want to build careers of their own can't because their husbands' companies keep transferring them to new locations where it means the wife has to seek new employment once again. Sometimes she has to move to isolated areas or bedroom communities where there are few jobs available. The husband may be asked to travel for days at a time from their new location. He does not miss as much the original family nucleus from where they were transferred because he is busy with his business where he has instant contact with his co-workers. His wife may be isolated in her new home. If he has to travel he may have opportunities to route his business trips over his old home town. For the wife and family, unless they are wealthy, these trips home can realistically be afforded only once a year.

If the mother works "to keep out of mischief" while the husband travels, the children suffer if there is no extended family to replace the working parents. The trend for mother to be out of the house is growing every year. In 1965, according to the U.S. census, 23.3% of married mothers with children under six worked. The most recent statistics tell us 36.6% (a 13.3% increase) of mothers with children under six work. In many households such lifestyles succeed. When the family is together, they are close and have a meaningful time together. The mother's working hours may be such that it coincides with the nursery school or day care center or she may work just once or twice a week.

For other families, it does not work out. If the father is not at home because he works late hours or he travels and it is hard to get steady and capable sitters, the mother is forced to stay home. If she resents having to stay home, the children will not get the patient loving care they need. Unfortunately, there are few day care centers available, especially in middle-class areas. Furthermore, there are many doubts among parents as to how good day care centers are for children under two and one-half years old. Very young children may need a one-to-one relationship they can count on until they are old enough to take care of basic immediate needs. There are many variables in life, and we can rarely make blanket statements. But, in general, if very young children do not have security, they may develop, in different degrees, anxiety, excessive clinging habits, fear, learning difficulties, hyperactivity, and in adult years, excessive dependency needs and a poor ability to form close relationships.

More and more mothers realize the importance of steady and loving care and are solving the problem by making arrangements with another stay-at-home mother with pre-school-age children to care for her children while she is at work.

If the family should move back to the extended family, the older children have not enough in common with the cousins because they have no memories of sharing experiencees and fun while they are children. What all this "daddy traveling," "mother keeping busy out of the home," and the whole family moving up and onward but away from the cousins, aunts, uncles, and grand-parents can do to a family is well-portrayed by the following history told by Jennifer F., a woman executive, at an all women's self-help meeting. It is an important story because it is so very typical of our new and prevalent lifestyle.

Case History: Jennifer F.
"I was taught by my mother that it is fine to be independent

and competitive. The reason my mom taught me that is because Dad moved about a lot in his executive position. She thought she would make up for the loneliness by preaching independence. But it did not make up for the warmth and security I needed. I felt alienated and insecure away from aunts, uncles, cousins, and grandparents. We associated with all kinds of people to be social and help Dad up the ladder. Mom didn't work, but she kept busy by playing cards every afternoon with a group of women who sipped sherry while together. Mom gave the image of a woman who would do no more than nag if she wanted something or was unhappy about Dad's traveling. Never did she show anger or competitiveness. In her eyes, the ideal woman shows to the world cheerfulness, a cute helplessness, and seductiveness even if she has to drink to manage the image. Mom did drink heavily as the years went on. And when she drank, she was pleasant. She said my life would be different that hers. But all that Mom taught me about being able to do anything I wanted to, I soon learned was not necessarily accepted by society and the opportunities in many towns we stayed in were nil. Many girls avoided success in these towns to prove their femininity. Those women who made it big career-wise always camouflaged their success with exaggerated femininity. At the same time, I was torn between wanting to be accepted by the local people and local boys and wanting to be a sophisticated successful career woman. Drinking helped."

These themes that run through this case history show us how a lack of family life, a lack of a proper mother model, and a father dominated by business confused the woman and complicated her drinking problems.

Women are looking at their lives in greater depths. Treatment centers that are helping women to stop drinking use consciousness-raising methods. A counselor in one co-ed treatment center in Massachusetts said, "We find the fastest way to get a woman to stand on her own two feet is to make her aware of the fact that marriage, the old-fashioned lifestyle, may not be for her." A few years ago, if a woman did not "fit" into a set female image, she had no alternative."

The same treatment center said outright, "Those of our women who got divorced recovered better than those who went back to their problems." Of course, it does not say much for their marriages in the first place or the types of homes they came from.

Feminism Does Not Cause Alcoholism

It seems clear by now that feminism alone does not cause alcoholism. It always takes a combination of circumstances to cause alcoholism. And among the factors that make up this combination of problems, if we are to term them modern, are the higher divorce rate (break up of family), the husband/father who is too often absent or who lacks understanding of a woman's needs, and lack of contact with the extended family. If a woman's life is not running smoothly because of abuse, poverty physical problems, etc., it obviously will not do to try to place all the blame on whether she stays home or works. As a matter of fact, working may open horizons that will help her to grow away from her problems.

According to the feminists, the woman who stays home to take care of her small children, household, and family in general which often includes retired and elderly relatives, works as hard as any career woman, perhaps even harder since her work may include night-time nursing. Certainly, we can say that women alcoholics who stay home to raise children and women alcoholics who work outside the home are both working women with heavy responsibilities. Some, whether working in or outside the home, use alcohol to cope with divorce, separation from the extended family, and other stresses. Feminism is trying to help women solve these problems by suggesting, for instance, that men take paternal leave from work in case of family crisis. This may include the birth of a new baby or a mother feeling ill. Feminism is suggesting that the family work together, and in the case of a single woman without brothers or sisters, that the woman join a women's consciousness-raising group so that she is not alone with her problems.

Looking Backward to Today

A quick glance back through the pages of literature will give us a fresh perspective from which to view the problem of alcohol and women. Certainly, it will remind us that tipsy ladies are by no means a new phenomenon. F. Scott Fitzgerald's chic leading ladies are very much at home with alcohol and drunkenness. In John O'Hara's book, *From The Terrace*, the mother of the main character is an alcoholic literally imprisoned under the care of a nurse.

Neither is the woman of yesterday with a drinking problem limited to the pages of fiction. Richard B. Sewall in his *The Life of Emily Dickinson*, the biography of the famous American poetess and recluse (1830–1886), tells about Emily's sister-in-law, Sue Gilbert Dickinson, who created a "wretched, raving, chaotic" life for the family because of her alleged alcoholism (supposedly inherited from her father). Sue had "fits" which made her husband's life unbearable. Of course, he did have a mistress, but most people in town understood that. According to the old journals (written in the 1880s), Sue had a "morbid dread of having any children." She looked upon sex as "low practices" and did everything in her power to have her pregnancies aborted.

Another interesting woman is Samuel Johnson's first wife. Samuel Johnson (1709–1784), famous English poet, critic and man of letters, was known for his peevishness and arrogance. He himself was untidy, but of his wife, he demanded perfection when it came to housekeeping and cooking. He himself would go to the coffee house with his friends and leave her home to do her chores. Instead, the dear lady drank and died an alcoholic.

When one reads the histories of such women as Sue Dickinson and Mrs. Samuel Johnson, one asks, is there honestly a rise in women alcoholics, or has women's lib given the women the courage to come out of their houses and say, "Look, I have a problem."

Radio and television are also helping alcoholics to face their problems by talking about alcoholism and by interviewing both male and female alcoholics.

Many counselors who have seen housewives get depressed when their children left the nest point out that a good job and sessions at a women's consciousness-raising group may be a salvation. When questioned, many housewives admitted that they drank because they were bored to tears. This is especially true of wives whose husbands get moved from city to city. He is busy, and she feels uprooted. Too many wives drink because while not using their talents they doubt their own worth as their husbands move forward in their careers. Statistics bear out that females are less inclined to be involved in habitual drinking while also maintaining their employment.

Whatever the psychological reasons may have been for such people as Mrs. Samuel Johnson or Sue Dickinson's behavior, today's attitude would permit such women to pursue a different lifestyle. The alternatives are many today and can open a whole new world of hope to the alcoholic woman.

Updates
- Career women sometimes rationalize uncontrolled drinking with such thoughts as "My job is dull or I don't get the credit I deserve." Science Daily reported in 2014 a study tracking alcohol use and career prospect. It indicated that a declining career was the result of alcohol use rather than signaling that participants developed substance use disorders as a result of a frustrating work life.
- "It isn't my drinking that damaged my marriage. It's that my husband didn't appreciate my education, my talent, my career," is another rationalization that successful women use to drink. Men do have inferiority complexes and may act out inappropriately. However, among the well adjusted men attitudes toward educated, successful women have changed. Beginning in the mid-1980s, women's college completion rates began to exceed men's, and their educational advantage has continued to grow since then, showing no signs of slowing. (Schwatz and Han) Among couples who married in the 1990s or later, a wife's educational advantage over her husband was no longer associated with an increased risk of divorce. Furthermore the gender difference in household chores is increasingly leveling.

- Unfortunately employers do not pay enough attention to women who are alcohol abusers. Alcoholism reduces productivity and therefore contributes to a company's costs. SAMHSA reported that in 2004 to 2008 a study showed that among the nearly 50 million women age 18 to 64 who were employed full time, 9.9 million engaged in binge drinking (19.8 percent). Only 1.2 percent of these heavy drinking women were referred to treatment by their employer or human services. Most were referred by the criminal justice system after having been stopped or arrested for driving under the influence. Many of these binge drinkers manage to go undetected or are in a workplace which chooses to ignore the problem.
- Those who manage to arrest their drinking and concentrate on their careers, productivity, and goals, tend to be happier, healthier and have more friends than those who continue to drink. The Terman Study (defined in chapter 6 in this book) notes that "—level of education was not a strong predictor of later health and longevity—. Rather, it was—perseverance, and the patterns of accomplishments—"

CHAPTER 9

THE CULTURAL STRESS FACTOR: I

Not all of the stress in the life of the drinking woman is to be traced to the tensions arising out of her feminism, her marriage, her family, or her sexuality. There are cultural stresses still to be explored. These are the particular stresses experienced by the black woman, for example, as a result of her unique heritage and present situation, in distinction to those she experiences simply as "woman." They are the stresses experienced by the women of Appalachia as they have moved from the farm to the city. Or the breaking up of an old culture as the Indian and Eskimo women have experienced it. We are talking about lonely women senior citizens who never drank in their active years, but who do so now because they cannot cope in an uncaring society that inflicts them with inflation, crime, pollution, noise, and overcrowding. We are talking about the pain and guilt sometimes involved in intermarriages, or the fear and the guilt that may build up within us when we abandon a religion or a culture.

Joan's Story

This factor of cultural stress can be clearly seen in Joan's story. Joan, a black woman, talked to her counselor in her treatment center in meaningful terms for our purposes.

Joan said, "I doubt if I'll stop drinking when I get out of here. What have I got to look forward to? Originally, I came from the South to New York City because I heard the jobs were better here. Back home we were very poor tenant farmers. The dirt around our shanty was our kitchen garden. I had never seen a real bathroom until I came to New York. Our social life was the church. Once I got to New York, I found out that there is nothing I know how to do. I have burlgarized, I have prostituted myself because there is nothing I can do. Sometimes I don't even understand what people are trying to explain to me. I have taken a few jobs cleaning homes, but I keep losing those jobs. I drift from one job to the other. At home, even if you haven't got a job, there are always chores that have to be done leaving little time for drink. In the city, if you have a job, it lasts eight hours and then you can spend the rest of the time drinking. I live in an area where the rats outnumber people. I watch the neighborhood kids meet dope peddlers whether they want to or not. I can't go back home because I am ashamed of how I have lived. My family back home are Baptists. They don't drink. My counselor here says one problem is I never learned to drink, and I feel guilty every time I drink. I say, I feel blue and strung out, why shouldn't I drink?"

What Joan reports is supported by many studies. When confronted by the stresses produced by over-population, extreme poverty, poor diet, or a breakdown in the immediate and extended family unit, a woman may learn to use alcohol as a coping mechanism. It is these cultural stresses that deserve to be looked at in greater detail. In many cases, these women are the forgotten and ignored alcoholics. To understand them, we must look separately at the stresses of each cultural group.

The Black Woman in the Slums

Alcoholism is the number one health problem in black urban communities. It is directly related to crime, unemployment, broken families, child abuse, fear, inferior feelings, and a sense of anger. Alcohol is a fast and short-lived ego booster. It is also a way of numbing one's senses against an intolerable job. If unemployed or staying home with small children, it is a way of passing the day.

Pettigrew, in a study entitled, Blacks in the Liquor Industry, points out that while black Americans buy 30% of the scotch in America, they receive little, if any, benefits from the profits they are pouring into the industry.

People in the slums are not to be confused with their brethren who have entered the middle class. The pattern of drinking among the black American middle class does not vary greatly from the white middle class.

The Black Woman's History

The fate history has imposed on the black American woman has given her a unique outlook on life. Let's look at some of that history. To blacks belongs the distinction of being the only people who were forced to come to these shores. Ripped away unexpectedly from country and mother, sometimes still as a child, the black woman never knew her background, her family, or the strengths of her culture. What she learned, she learned mostly from the white slave owner, or by word of mouth from fellow blacks.

The black woman is essentially a strong woman who has had to do what she could to survive. Often it meant being the breadwinner. This has been the theme of many popular and biographical novels. Gordon Parks, in his book, *The Learning Tree*, describes his mother as a strong, hard-working black woman whose final wish on this earth was that her son leave the South and go up north where she hoped he could make something of himself. Lorraine Hansberry in *A Raisin in the Sun* depicted the mother as a strong leader within a family beset by social bigotry. From where did these black women get their internal strength?

The black woman is as strong as she is because from the day she set foot on these shores, she was not shielded and protected from rape, from hard work, from ill health, or from drinking parties as was the white woman, by the church, a family unit, and by social ethics. From her earliest days in this country, the only medicine she knew against pain and illness was alcohol. The slave owners also used alcohol as a means of controlling their slaves. The masters gave alcohol to the slaves during the holidays and other leisure periods to stifle all thoughts of running away or rebelling.

Life was not much better after the Civil War. During the Reconstruction Era, many states in the South passed laws prohibiting the possession of firearms or alcohol to the newly freed people. The white Southerner knew black Americans had much about which to be angry and feared that without the structures and institutions of slavery alcohol would free their inhibited anger. To many black people, these laws were only another indication that they were not fully free, and they would drink all the more to assert their right to full freedom.

Where segregation rigorously limited black access to public recreation, the "Negro" tavern offered recreation and a breather from the daily problems. Only the church offered an alternative possibility for family recreation. When the Depression and Second World War produced the migration of black to northern urban areas in search of high-paying jobs, they were a people who had had much experience with the alcohol as a coping mechanism.

The urban area with its street subcultures of hustling, gambling, bars, rent parties and fast money offered a new lifestyle, and a new pattern of drinking. The black woman was seduced into this lifestyle as much as the men. She worked in factories, she went to bars and she chipped in and drank her share at the rent parties. She did not feel self-conscious if she got high at these parties because, except for the church it was her only recreation. She went as openly to the taverns as the men. Still today, in the tavern one hears about the available jobs, the latest gossip. Here the black women makes transactions, and borrows or lends money.

The Drinking Black Woman
It is against the background of this history that the drinking of the black ghetto woman must be seen.

A study done by Stern and Pittman finds that, as might be expected, black ghetto women who drink heavily do not drink for the same reasons as do their middle-class sisters. Their middle-class sisters drink because of boredom or because they have a low esteem of themselves or come from less happy homes than their nondrinking neighbors. Poor black people have no time for such middle-class introspective thoughts.

THE DRINKING WOMAN: REVISITED

The poor black woman lives in a state of ambiguity. Far from worrying why Daddy seemed to love her sister more, she may not even know who her father was. She may not know where her present husband is, nor may she be able to provide her children with the knowledge of who their father was or where he is.

This ambiguity has taken its toll on the black woman. On the one hand, she has had to put up with prejudice. She has been relegated, as one eloquent patient in a treatment center expressed it, "to clean most of the world's toilets," so she can support her family. Because she has had to take on a greater burden than the men in the family, she has, in some cases, developed a role confusion in her life. How many jobs should she take on mothering, fathering, nursing, child-bearing and breadwinning? What can she do when her husband walks out because he can't tolerate his ineffectualness as a man? Is it any wonder that many black women have a poor self-image and feelings of inadequacy?

The black woman drinks also because she is too exhausted from the overcrowded tenements and too tense from the inevitable, ubiquitous noise. She has a low esteem, not of herself, but of her people as seen by whites. Her neighbors and. family understand why she drinks. They don't necessarily look down on her as a middle-class family would if one of theirs drank. The poor black people are more permissive because they have more compassion. Seldom does a poor black woman feel abandoned by her family as a middle-class woman would because of her drinking.

The poor black woman also drinks because she is angry. Joan, whom we met in the beginning of this chapter, once told her counselor that all she felt was anger— "anger at my folks for not preparing me for this shit life, anger for the city for treating me like dirt, and anger at myself for putting up with it."

As we will see when we come to consider the American Indians and the Eskimos, anger is a common denominator among all suppressed people. Yet even here, cultural differences leave their mark. Clara B. Synigal, Director of Interim House, a rehabilitation facility in Germantown, Pennsylvania, for women addicted to alcohol, has a sharp eye for the nuances of cultural problems and stresses. She notes, for example, that the Puerto Rican woman in the slums experiences much of the same ambiguity and anger as the black woman. And yet there are important differences in their drinking patterns. The Puerto Rican woman, she observes, "is generally not allowed to get treatment. Within the traditions of her cultural beliefs, she is supposed to be protected. She is not allowed to be around in mixed company, and she is not allowed to go to tap rooms and places of that sort. So she drinks in her home."

A Publically Accepted Pattern of Behavior

All of this means that for poor ghetto blacks in general, and for the poor black woman in particular, drinking has become a highly visible and acceptable pattern of behavior. Sterne and Pittman in *Drinking Patterns in the Ghetto* note that ghetto children are accustomed to seeing drinking in the park, the courtyards of the public projects, or in front of the small private buildings. The streets are littered with beer cans and liquor bottles. The curious child whose parents may not be able to provide supervision will pick up the containers and taste the few remaining drops. The drunks are heard and smelled. The excitement from the local taverns oozes out into the streets. It is known that the local junk man, always a curiosity to children, gives the garbageman and the maintenance men from the projects a bottle of inferior wine in exchange for salvaging saleable items. Piri Thomas in his autobiographical novel, *Down These Mean Streets*, confirms this general characterization of the ghetto subculture.

Moreover, Sterne and Pittman made it clear that youngsters learn at an early age how to cope with the drinking patterns of adults. A mother who has been summoned to the police station regarding a fight between her sons, aged ten and thirteen, and two other children, arrives drunk, disheveled and very belligerent. The younger son appears to be very embarrassed by his mother's behavior; the older one is instructed to take her home.... An eight-year-old girl, responding to a TAT card (Thematic Apperception Test), tells a story about a mother who goes to a tavern near the project while her husband is at work and her children are at school, drinks "wine and beer," drinks "too much" and becomes "dizzy" and "drunk" and then wants to "go home and lay down." Some men bring her home and "beat her up," presumably because they did not want her to leave the tavern at that time. The child is uncertain about the interpersonal motivations behind the assault, but it is very clear that she regards her mother as providing an acceptable female role model for alcohol use. She also indicates how one may cope with intoxication: go home, "lay on the bed and take some aspirins and go to sleep." A twelve-year-old girl knows that "beer makes Mommy sick." A thirteen-year-old girl, searching through a drawer of papers and envelopes, explains that she is looking for some money her mother hid: "My mama was drunk when she came in last night and when she's like that she usually puts her money in an envelope or something. She told me that if I found it, to go out and buy groceries and buy a pair of shoes for myself."

The Black Adolescent Female

Meantime, the black adolescent female has developed her own patterns of alcohol abuse, particularly if she has dropped out of school. In such reports as that by Sterne and Pittman, it is indicated that dropouts like to emulate adult behavior. Drinking is the ideal activity, the initiation into the adult world. Drink offers success in interpersonal relationships. You are your own best publicity agent if you get arrested and defy the "system." Male adolescents in the ghetto tend to drink in male groups. Female adolescents in the ghetto tend to drink heterosexually. At a young age, an adolescent will be careful how much she drinks because she wants to protect herself sexually. If a young man offers a young woman wine, he is "cheap." Whiskey and scotch, just like the ads on TV and in the slick magazines, have status, and when a young man offers her such a drink, he's trying to impress her. To seem sophisticated, a young woman will often pretend that she is on her third drink while she is actually on her first. One very young woman in a treatment center who had lived in a housing project, explained it this way, "If you drink too much, it can affect your chances of making a good marriage. If you don't drink at all, it can keep you from meeting anyone whatsoever."

Those girls who are not afraid of getting pregnant, who do not see themselves as being taken advantage of in casual sexual encounters with boys, drink as much as their dates. Many young people today have early sexual relations. However, girls in the ghetto are less protected than middle-class girls. Those raised by religious families may feel intense guilt.

The black woman's ghetto family gives her, in many cases, a great amount of sexual freedom. She is not made to feel unloved as her white sister is for becoming pregnant out of wedlock. Nor is she pushed into an abortion as are many of her middle-class sisters. Her mother, grandmother, great-grandmother will care over the baby. The teenage fathers of these babies do not always take their responsibility seriously. However, this is beginning to change. More and more black men are breaking this pattern and concerning themselves that their sons not fall into it.

The women accept that the very young men are expected to be sexually exploitive and know that they are rated by their peers for it.

It is not unusual for an adolescent woman to have a baby by the time she is fifteen. While the elders watch the baby, she stands outside smoking and drinking with her peers. Other 13-year-olds may be admiring her. She has at least done something with her life. Had she abstained from drinking, sex, pregnancy, she would be nothing but another plain school dropout, whose reading and writing is questionable. She has distinguished herself from her small group of peers.

The Single Parent

Once a dropout has had a baby, she does not necessarily continue to drink. Many divorced and separated women in the ghetto abstain from alcohol, especially if receiving welfare. These women have a fear that their social worker may take their child away (Tamerin, Neumann and Marshall, 1971). If she drinks, she will do so in the tavern where she will be less apt to be seen by her social worker. She has discovered that the urban life offers her, if she wants it, greater anonymity than the Southern rural life did.

Sterne and Pittman say that the older women in the ghetto drink more inside in relatives' homes and men, more outdoors on the streets and in the parks. Women will drink outdoors when they want to meet a man.

There are other reasons why the divorced or deserted woman may abstain from drinking. Alcohol may disgust her. A drinking husband may have broken up her marriage. If she is the wage earner, she cannot afford to drink.

We must be careful not to jump to the conclusion that all black women drink. According to Frederick Harper of Howard University, 49% of black women drink. He goes on to state in his book, *Alcohol Abuse and Black America*, that those who do not drink (51%) may have to take care of husbands who do have drinking problems. Others have been taught, especially if from the South, that nice ladies don't drink.

A black woman in the slums does not necessarily rely on her husband for support. (This is beginning to change. As we have stated earlier in this chapter, the black man is becoming aware of his identity.) In contrast to her white sister, if she is divorced, widowed, or a single parent, she is rarely lonely. Black people have larger families, live together, have ample church activities, neighbors, meet in the street and go to taverns, even when not drinking.

Understanding Counseling

Only now are we coming to understand the full complexity of providing adequate counseling for such a person as the black drinking woman. When she does seek help, she often is not comfortable with the helper's technical language, lifestyle, and goals. If the counselor is a white, middle-class person, as so many of the social workers are, she finds it difficult to relate life in the slums.

The late Fred T. Davis, a black and former field consultant of the National Council on Alcoholism, tried to make the helping professions aware that people can only relate to what their environment has shown them. Counselors in the treatment centers should be of the same ethnic background and preferably born and raised themselves in the slums. Only those who pulled themselves up by the boot straps can understand the lack of housing, education, and family breakdown. They will know how to explain the available resources (such as church, identification groups, physicians) within the immediate community.

The language of a psychiatrist, therapist, or counselor can be confusing. An indigenous staff puts the idea of seeking help on an understandable level. Such a counselor can give courage because she can say, "I grew up around the corner from you, and if I made it, you can make it."

The importance of letting a person know that she (or he) can change her life cannot be emphasized enough. Dr. Browne-Mayers, who is active in detoxification centers catering to the poor blacks, says, "So many have been raised on a poor diet, lived in cold tenements, and educated in a public school where they experienced failure (perhaps as young as first grade). The only defense left to such persons is apathy. Apathy is the greatest problem."

It is so difficult to cope efficiently under such circumstances that relapses are inevitable. A hospital or a detoxification center is not necessarily as we may think, the first step to recovery but only a chance to sleep in a clean bed and have a few meals. When the poor come out, they start drinking all over again because they don't know how to attain such living conditions on their own. This apathy, this helplessness must be pierced.

Fred T. Davis felt it was important for a counselor to distinguish whether a patient is playing games with him—"I can't get a job because I am black"—or has she truly trouble coping.

A counselor has to be versed in black history so that when family life is reestablished, the roots can go deeper and further back than America. Does she know how valuable family life was in Africa? A woman alcoholic has to know that family life is the foundation of sanity. The counselor cannot let the patient feel that her cure is synonymous with being a high school graduate. Programs can be worked out. There is nothing wrong in telling a patient it is all right to be whatever she or her husband can be. A patient has to realize that even if she or her husband earns little, family unity is her strength. Patients have to learn that parks, free concerts, museums can provide more fun than sitting in a tavern. And finally, the patient may have to be confronted about her prejudice against white facilities, white counselors, and white employees.

This prejudice against the white can become a habit. The counselor has to help the patient distinguish what is prejudice against the black and what is constructively available for her in the white world.

One section of one chapter is hardly sufficient to describe the black people's history and present-day plight in the slums. What is known is that, given the history of alcohol use as medicine, alcohol to celebrate holidays, alcohol to keep people in one area, we have taught black America that the way to cope with poverty and tenements is to use alcohol and dope.

The Drinking Jewish Woman

The Jewish tradition, as it exists in contemporary America, was powerfully shaped by the Jewish experience in Europe. In this tradition, alcohol abuse was almost unheard of. A shikker (a drunk, in Yiddish) was considered a shame, something that could not exist among the Jewish people. Those rare families who did have a schicker pretended he or she wasn't there. In the old ghettos in Europe, there was a pressure to behave well, and the Jews tried to show their oppressors that they were worthy people. Loneliness rarely existed among the Jews in the ghetto because they all lived together and helped each other. A newcomer was always welcomed into a stranger's home and was invited by each household to share their meager meals. Little rooms were used as gathering places, and the rabbis were their leaders, comforters, and advisors. In order to cope with the harshness of the pogroms and the indignities of the ghetto, the Jews in Europe put their hearts into religion. Alcohol was used to celebrate religious festivals and not to cope with stress. The Jewish books of learning caution the people about alcohol. Isaiah, the prophet, warns of "morning drink."

In the United States, the Jewish alcoholic may be afraid to go to her rabbis or Jewish agencies because alcoholism is considered a non-Jewish, problem. An alcoholic attending an Alcoholics Anonymous meeting in Central Synagogue in New York said that she still can't believe she is an alcoholic. Jews just aren't alcoholics. She said it would never have occurred to her to find out what Alcoholics Anonymous is or to go to an Alcoholics Anonymous meeting in a church because church meant Christian to her. It was her rabbi who finally guided her into Alcoholics Anonymous. She was originally of Orthodox background and such a woman, even though she may not practice her religion, feels guilty entering a church.

In "Impressions of Jewish Alcoholics," an article by W. Schmidt and R. E. Popham, it is explained that little has been done to understand the relatively small number of Jewish alcoholics that do exist. In this same study, the caseworker noted that the Jewish alcoholic she met showed guilt feelings of disgrace that he as a Jew could be an alcoholic. If a Jewish man feels this way, it must be twice as hard for a woman. One Jewish woman said, "When I was in the hospital for an operation, I told my anesthetist that I am an alcoholic. His answer was, 'I don't believe it—a nice Jewish girl like you.'"

The Breakdown Of A Tradition

It is increasingly the case, however, that Jews in America are not dependent on the Jewish community for their survival. Religion is becoming purely a voluntary function in their lives. With the loosening of religious ties has come a loosening of the total context of life and culture, including the use of alcohol. Jewish grandparents and parents saw no need to educate their children how to drink because to them drinking was mostly part of the numerous blessings in the Jewish religious ceremonies, and they did not foresee that their children might not follow the old traditions.

Some Jews began to participate in heavy drinking as they joined the American armed services or went to college. The Jewish woman, as she dated Jewish men, copied him to be sophisticated and socially worthy of him. The families who succeeded and moved into suburbia's cocktail circuit have in some cases crossed the line to alcoholism. Jewish women invited to country clubs or club luncheons have a drink at noon already if only "to belong." In the meantime, their husbands may be having several drinks in town with business clients.

Although the Jewish population has fewer alcoholics than other segments of our population, alcoholism is increasing among them.

There was a time when hotels, country clubs, and caterers used to moan that Jewish customers meant a big loss at the bar. Not anymore. Liquor flows at Bar Mitzvahs, Bas Mitzvahs, and weddings. Kosher hotels keep their bars well stocked for their customers. A Reform temple in Westchester County in New York sends out yearly notices to its members ". . . 'grownups' of our new families have been invited to a social evening of cocktails, dinner. . . ."

If a Jewish man gets shikker, it is laughed off, especially if it is a happy occasion. It is inconceivable that a Jewish woman could get intoxicated at any occasion. A Jewish woman is surrounded by laws that are designed to keep her chaste, faithful and basically, a good mother. If she drinks, her guilt is twice as bad as that of a Jewish man.

As the authors of *The Jewish Woman In America* put it, the Jewish woman in America is part of a 3,500-year-old religious and historical tradition. These traditional Jewish attitudes shape her self-image still today at the very deepest level and cause men to see her in a certain image. They put the Jewish woman in a special place. And they influence her cultural stresses. One of these ancient laws states that a woman must not have contact with a man while she is menstruating. Such a tradition cannot but have a profound effect on the woman searching to come to terms with herself as a biological being. When these laws were made over three millenniums ago, blood was considered with fear and repugnance. Even if the Reform and Conservative Jews have dropped these laws, their Orthodox brethren practice them, and they are still very much a part of the Jewish consciousness today.

These same laws lay a heavy burden on the Jewish husband in his behavior toward his wife. One example is to be found in the *Code of Maimonides Book Four: The Book of Women* where it is stated ". . . (if) he is affluent enough to free his wife from nursing, and if she is unwilling to nurse, he must, even if he has no handservant, hire a wet nurse or purchase a maid servant, because a woman can only rise in status with her husband and not descend."

The modern Jew has rebelled intellectually against all such laws. He may not even know these laws—and there are many who share this ignorance—but their feeling, flavor, and tradition remains.

A Jewish woman who has been deserted by her husband because he "can now afford something better" in his upward mobile liberated life, may, in her helplessness and confusion, sit home and drink. Many Jewish women have low feelings about themselves to begin with. If her husband has walked out on her—or even if she has walked out on him for some reason—and if she is away from home, from her community, may feel terribly lost. She may not want to get back to her community. She may be rebelling against herself. She may be angry because she may have heard many negative statements about women not only from her husband but from her father too, rooted in such ghetto sayings as, "Many daughters, many troubles."

The Case Of Iris

Iris is a Jewish girl who became an alcoholic and died of an overdose of tranquilizers and alcohol. She was a very talented fabric designer. Her parents urged her to get married because it wasn't becoming for a Jewish girl to stay single. She married a pilot who wanted her full attention when he was home but expected her to "keep busy" while he was out of town. The marriage for many other reasons did not work out and ended in divorce. In the eyes of her tradition-minded family, it was all her fault. By not acting appropriately, she had not made him happy. Without even verbalizing it, they communicated to her their deep disappointment.

But her career was getting along nicely. She was asked out often by her colleagues and she felt liberated having a drink for lunch, another after work, and one before and after dinner. When she was not with people, she drank and didn't eat. One New Year's Eve, she didn't have a date. She didn't feel comfortable calling her family to ask them what they were doing. Instead, she decided a few valiums and a few drinks would give her a good night's sleep. It did—permanently.

Her death wasn't her husband's fault. Something in her tradition and in her upbringing did not teach her to cope. She couldn't go home anymore, and she couldn't seek help. She had never worked out her cultural stress.

Other Jewish women talk about having wonderful husbands, but are not able to cope with the drinking society they meet within their community. "I was like a child newly liberated in a penny candy store who couldn't control herself," was how one woman explained her alcoholism. "I also had abandoned my Jewish culture," she added, "and I guess when you give up a culture, you try to replace it with something new. I wanted to be a modern WASP. It didn't work. Alcohol didn't work for a lot of my WASP friends either who were drinking too heavily." Most women, however, talk about drinking by themselves and not feeling comfortable about drinking excessively in public.

There is a sense in which these problems are not unique to the Jewish woman. However, there is a subtle difference. The Jewish woman has never been able to rebel like her Christian sister because she has been busy coping with anti-Semitism. Even in the United States, she has been aware of the holocaust and the long history of indignities against her people, that she has been afraid to expose her feelings for fear that she would supply fuel to the world's anti-Semitism.

The Urban Jewish Woman
These two factors—the breaking down of the old Jewish tradition, and the ever-present deep-seated fear of anti-Semitism—have affected the Jew of the urban slums as well, and have created new pressures for the use of alcohol. In the old days, there was a tightly knit community which gave support to the individual. Today, Jewish people who live in slums or in housing projects, and who are lonely and who cannot afford recreation, sit home in front of the TV and may drink just like "the beautiful and successful people" portrayed in the liquor advertisements. Jews who live in lower-middle-class areas have pressures from which they seek relief. They are afraid to go out at night because of crime. They may have brought certain paranoid fears with them from Europe but cannot afford a psychiatrist. Among these people may be Jews who have been in concentration camps and who do not have any family left and who find no comfort in their religion. They deal with their deep feelings of aloneness and rejection by drinking. Some may feel guilty that they were spared. The memory of watching their brothers and sisters being taken away while they remained needs to be anesthetized.

One alcoholic woman in New York City said she had lost all her relatives in the holocaust. An agency had brought her and her mother over to the United States before the holocaust. She never married. She took care of her mother. When her mother died, she never again felt close to anyone. She now had a job putting price tags on clothes. All day long she sits and stamps them on. On weekends, she is invited to join friends, but she is afraid to go out alone and, in desperation, she drinks.

There are, comparatively speaking, very few Jewish alcoholics. Jews have been known to take dope and be heavy smokers. Doris H. Milman, M.D., and Wen Huey Su, M.A., in Patterns of Drug Use

Among University Students (1973), have noted a correlation between marijuana intake and Jewish background. But our youth in general has discovered that alcohol is legal and cheaper and easier to get than dope. And increasingly there is no reason for the Jewish girl in high school or in college to act differently than the other students.

Jewish women alcoholics tend not to show up in the statistics of the public hospitals. Many refuse to give their religion when they enter a hospital because they are ashamed. But the rabbis are beginning to see them in those synagogues which have opened their doors to Alcoholics Anonymous. One sees them at cocktail parties. One hears old Alcoholics Anonymous members talk about how they are noticing Jewish people at AA meetings who they never noticed before. One hears of them going to private clinics. If you walk among alcoholics, they are there. Dr. Stanley Gitlow, clinical professor of medicine at Mt. Sinai Medical School in New York City, and an internist specializing in alcoholism, says that when he first started his practice there were fewer Jewish alcoholics who came for help, and those who did come, were sicker than the non-Jewish alcoholic. Today, he noted, there are more Jewish people seeking help for alcoholism. They are not necessarily sicker than the non-Jewish alcoholics, and in his practice, the Jewish woman is not uncommon.

It is time for those Jewish women who are alcoholics to come to terms with their peculiar stresses. And, above all, it is time to stop being ashamed. An illness is no disgrace.

Updates
- More African American women are affiliated with a church than African American men. The church provides social, spiritual and financial resources. Many African Americans are affiliated with the Baptist church which preaches abstinence (Herd 1996, Taylor et al. 1999) which has contributed to a low alcoholism rate among African American women.
- According to a survey completed in 2005 Hispanic women who were willing to answer questions in English rather than in Spanish admitted to a higher rate of alcohol consumption than those who were only able to answer in Spanish. We can

assume from this survey that Hispanic women who have accepted their new culture in the United States are heavier drinkers than those who maintain their homeland culture. (Pearson et al.2009)

CHAPTER 10

THE CULTURAL STRESS FACTOR: II

Indians
Indian women make up another group that has been sadly neglected and misunderstood.

Much has been said about the Indian people and alcohol, and much of it is nonsense. It has been said that the Indian who once has tasted liquor, has an uncontrollable craving for it forever after and always loses control over personal behavior when drinking. There is a record of a Nevada Supreme Court case, circa 1906, in which the judge solemnly noted that the defendants mentioned in their briefs that it is generally known that alcohol destroys more so the mental faculties of the Indian than of the white man. No proof for this generalization is cited. On the other hand, Jerold E. Levy and Stephen J. Kunitz, in their book, *Indian Drinking, Navajo Practices and Anglo-American Theories*, remind us that the long warfare the Indian experienced with the white man was very disorganizing, and wars do produce disorganization, debauchery, and acculturation.

It is not even known how many Indians drink. There are many statistics, some quite discouraging, but nothing completely definite. The Indian is spread about the country, many are half-breeds, some have left the reservations and others live off by themselves and don't encourage researchers to join them. Bert P. Eder, a Sioux from the Ft. Peck Reservation, Montana, stated in Alcohol Health and Research World that the rate of alcoholism among Indians closely parallels that of the nation. He also noted that no proof exists that the psychological reaction of Indians to alcohol is any more severe than that of other racial groups.

On the other hand, a recent article in Alcohol Health and Research World maintained that alcoholism is at present the number one health problem among all Indians and their ethnic relatives, the Eskimos. In 1973, the National Institute of Mental Health said that 75–80% of all suicides among Indians are alcohol related, a rate that exceeds by two or three times that of our general population. In 1972, the National Center for Health Statistics said the three fastest rising causes of death among Indians, in order of frequency, were cirrhosis of the liver, suicide, and homicide. All three obviously can be traced to destructive tendencies.

This same report estimates that Indian drinking is double that of the general population, and underlies a significantly larger proportion of suicides, homicides, criminal acts, traffic accidents, and acts of violence committed by Indians.

Alcohol Use And Abuse Among The Indians

Whatever the statistical picture may finally turn out to be, our knowledge of the history of the American Indian since the coming of the white man should remind us of the cultural stresses her life experience had placed on the Indian woman whom we have stereotyped into a beaded squaw doll.

To understand the drinking of the Indian woman, we have first to examine the use of alcohol by the Indians as a group. While some Indians, at least, made alcohol from corn and cactus, it was used primarily for spiritual purposes. It was the white man who introduced the use of alcohol to enhance the treaty and trading rights he wanted to negotiate. The chiefs drank when trading with the fur traders or with a spokesman for the whites. Some historians have maintained that the white man would have been unwilling to trade without alcohol since he knew he could get the better bargain if the Indian was under the influence of alcohol.

It was the white people who later on passed legislation prohibiting liquor traffic among the Native Americans. Although the law meant well, it smacked of discrimination and condescension. Indians nevertheless managed to obtain liquor. Indians who lived in the timber country and who worked mostly with the lumberjacks, a heavy drinking lot themselves, got their liquor illegally from them. Since the Indian could not be seen drinking while this law was in effect, he often drank in rapid gulps. The law was finally repealed in 1953.

Today there are Indian treatment centers catering to the Indian's traditional feelings. Indians are reticent not only with "outsiders" but even with an all-Indian group. Indians talk best with known and tried friends or a trusted counselor, sometimes a fellow Indian, who understands their need to be accepted as an Indian.

Many Indian treatment programs consider two elements important: spirituality and timelessness. In contrast to non-Indian treatment programs, a predetermined schedule is low-keyed while importance is placed on attuning a client to nature, and to ethical and religious values in relation to herself. Researchers, medical doctors and psychologists, have discovered that the Indian woman is reticent to share any knowledge she has about her peoples' alcoholism with the white researcher because, in part, the Indians do not trust whites.

Drink helps to loosen the tribal social constraints and the Indian's confusion about the white people's culture. The confusion includes a lack of identification with the common purpose of our society as a whole and a rejection of its goals. The consequence is a failure of social integration and constructive control of angry feelings.

Indian Children And Alcohol Abuse

The confusion and drinking starts early. Drinking is high among the boys and girls in the Indian Bureau of Indian Affairs Boarding School. The first few years of their lives, many Indians live on the reservation. If they go to "boarding schools" for Indians run by the Government, they are required to renounce their reservation style of life. They must, for example, cut their hair and wear different clothes. They are asked not to speak their own language, only English. Those Indians who go to the public school are frequently not in a much better position. Many live ten miles or more from the school bus stop, and will have a two-hour trip each way on the school bus once they reach the stop. Some public schools serving the Indian population do have a bilingual system, but it often is unsatisfactory. There never seem to be enough Indian teachers on the staff. Some Indian parents pay private families who live near the school to let their children "board" with them. Often these children are then subjected to the cross-cultural stress which arises when well-meaning families try to teach them "better" ways.

The Indians who are aware that their talents are doubly ripened by their own and the white people's culture are frustrated and angry that their talents go unused. The anger grows from youth on, but their elders caution them not to show their anger or show in public what they think and feel. The Indians believe that a show of emotion in public is equal to a loss of self-respect.

The Drinking Indian Woman

The Inter-Tribal Alcoholism Center in Sheridan, Wyoming, reported that approximately 25% to 35% of its clients are women. This center suspects that because of the Indian woman's family obligation, she is afraid to come for help. An Indian father will not do housework or, as a rule, take care of the children because he considers it unmanly and against the Indian tradition. The children would be neglected while she is out seeking help, and therefore, she is afraid that the social welfare department will take her children and place them in a foster home or put them up for adoption. The Indians call this "legal kidnapping."

If the Indian woman drinks, it is, at this point of our knowledge, surmised that she is copying a family pattern. Her father was as dissatisfied as her husband is today, and she bears the brunt of their unhappiness. She, as they, may seek relief in alcohol.

The Indian woman is exposed to many problems. One of them is earning a living on the reservation as well as off. It is here that we see the true tragedy of the Indian woman and alcohol abuse.

If an Indian woman decides to leave the reservation, her opportunities to earn money are limited, but her need for money, rent, and food are great. While she may be literate and capable of discussing her plight, her education is not always sufficient to cope away from the reservation. She may be burdened with illegitimate children since there is a tribal breakdown of regulatory mores. It is not unusual for her to be promiscuous to gain clothing, money, drink, or a trinket. She may prostitute herself for money. Most of her pickups take place in the local tavern where she sits and, naturally drinks. If she is arrested for vagrancy she becomes even more dependent.

Kuttner and Lorincz (1970) did a thorough study on promiscuity and prostitution as they found it on the skid row of Omaha, Nebraska, in Sioux City, Iowa (the nearest metropolitan area to the Omaha and Winnebago reservations), and in the Uptown district of Chicago. It is one of their main conclusions that alcohol abuse quickly becomes a part of the prostitute's sub-culture.

Indian women prefer to stay with fellow Indians, but since non-Indian and Indian "sections" adjoin each other in urban areas or in the small town, the non-Indian will often "rent quarters" to an Indian girl and hustle for her. When the Indian girl's man is in jail, it is not uncommon for her to hustle for herself.

She will get herself in the tavern early in the afternoon. Her hours are long, and she drinks to make it all bearable. She talks with the regular customers until the cattle raisers attending auctions, the farmers coming to market, or the pensioned men, laborers between jobs, or factory men between shifts, come in. Some workers, who get off the night shift at midnight or 8 A.M., go straight to the tavern.

A fight may ensue in the bar when a man tries to lure a girl away from the company she is with by offering a whole bottle instead of just drinks.

Weekends, she will have a reunion with her family in the Indian section of town. Drinking is by now a pattern in her life, and she will not abstain during her short reunion with her family. Her family will be of no help because the ones who are with her off the reservation may be alcoholics themselves, or so burdened that they are indifferent to her troubles. Those who could help her are geographically dispersed on the reservation.

The Plight Of The Half-Breed Woman

The situation of the half-breed is particularly difficult. Many tribes automatically reject half-breeds. They can't hold office; they are suspect of having contact with white families who would sell out the Indian. "Look out" is the constant watch word.

The half-breeds have to deal with cultural, religious, familial, and geographical upheavals. One such woman drank herself to death in Boston. The grandmother was a full Indian who married a Protestant rancher. The daughter of this marriage married a Catholic businessman in Chicago. The daughter of this Chicago union, who was now partly Indian, Catholic, Protestant, and white, met a Boston Jewish businessman of German descent who was visiting Chicago. She married, moved to Boston, and, for some reason, she did not practice any religion, never told her children about her Indian background, and did not pick up the meticulous German culture she had married into. She had low feelings about herself when she saw how her husband's family ran their tidy households.

Rather than bring out her culture or learn her husband's, she found it easier to drink. She never went back home to visit and never introduced her children to her Chicago, or Indian, family. It was only when she died and the families got together for her funeral that her children learned about their mother's Indian background. It's a pity that she did not live to see how excited and pleased her children were to learn about their heritage. There had been no need for her to make herself into a pariah.

Eskimos

Another group that has come to the attention of alcoholism experts are the Eskimos.

The Eskimos, when describing alcoholism, make few distinctions between male and female drinking. This may be because family life is set up in a tight unit. In an area where winter is extremely cold and winter nights are long and dark, homes are hard to keep warm and well-lighted. There may be no room for "private" or "secret" drinking, or for his or her activities. Many towns have only one recreation center. If there is only one recreation center in a town, drinking may be a common activity. One Eskimo nurse in Alaska related, "Eskimo youth is so used to sleeping in one room with the whole family that when they go off to boarding school in Seattle, they are very lonely."

Carol Molinari, who is director of the Center for Alcohol and Addiction Studies, University of Alaska, Anchorage, explained in Alcohol Health and Research World that the alcohol problem is compounded by the sociological changes being forced on the Eskimos as the white people spread their influence and culture into the Alaska wilderness. The pipeline has compounded the drinking problem. Now that the Alaskan natives have a high rate of pay, they can readily afford to drink. When the workers return to their native village for rest periods between tours of duty, they will often spend their money for spree drinking in which the entire village population is invited to take part. Among the Eskimos, as with other major sub-groups, we are beginning to recognize the importance of trained counselors from within the group.

Carol Molinari, obviously a woman with much compassion, explains how well the self-help approach works. A few years ago, a "do-it-yourself" campaign in behalf of alcoholism prevention struck a responsive chord in native communities across Alaska. One hundred seventy-one villages participated in a mini-grant program offered by the National Institute on Alcohol Abuse and Alcoholism. It gave villages the resources to combat local alcohol problems through small-scale community development of their own design. Grants up to $10,000 were awarded to each village applying with an acceptable plan.

Many of the qualifying villages used their grants to renovate or equip community centers. These centers then became the social and recreational gathering place. Often, they serve as the Alcoholics Anonymous meeting place as well. Such centers offer an alternative activity to drinking. They provide a place where alcohol information and health services can be administered. In Alaska's harsh climate such gathering places are often the only place available for social activities outside the home. In a remote village, these "do-it-yourselves" grants can mean a great deal.

Senior Citizens

Senior citizens comprise one of our most sadly neglected groups. Those senior citizens who abuse alcohol are noticed least because they are out of the mainstream of society. Recent statistics show there are 4.3 million older people living in households below the poverty threshold. Of these, nearly half were women, mostly widows living alone in a roominghouse setting. Almost half who live alone make do on less than $2,000 a year. Men have a greater chance to remarry than women and because there are more women than men, the widowers marry younger women. Even if they can afford a car, many women who are senior citizens today still belong to that generation in which women rarely learned to drive.

Problem drinking among the elderly is still limited. One obvious reason is that many active drinking alcoholics do not reach old age. Moreover, the majority of our present senior citizens were raised in a strong abstinence tradition (Ladies don't drink). Those older women who do drink are, therefore, very guilt-laden, especially if they can't control their drinking. And finally, many older people who were moderate-to-heavy drinkers decrease or stop drinking because of health.

Our new more open and liberated lifestyle means, however, that as each generation comes along a larger proportion of the women will almost certainly drink.

Since women live longer than men, they are more frequently forced to face loneliness. This is especially true of poor people who cannot afford to go out or to spend the carfare to visit friends and relatives. Should such a woman be living in a neighborhood new to her, she may be too timid to go out alone to meet people. Even if she lives within walking distance of a friend, she may be afraid of being criminally assaulted. For many of these women, even if they never were alcohol abusers, a cheap bottle of alcohol promises to anesthetize their dismal situation.

The very word "old age" or "retirement" is frightening. It is as if the senior citizens, many in excellent health, are leaving prematurely the world of the living. They are people whose pathological and biological infirmities are hurried along by their mode of living. For many of these people, there is little other amusement than a drink. If they live alone, drinking is easier than cooking. The children who may visit them don't say anything because drink is a way of controlling their parent. As long as Mom is "happy," why change her rhythm of life? Even if the children should succeed in getting her into Alcoholics Anonymous, someone would have to drive her to meetings.

The health agencies for the aged are too frequently "disgusted" by the female alcoholic and will try to pass her on to another agency who may refuse her because she is in the wrong category.

Alcoholism treatment centers exclude older people because they may become ill and have health problems not related to alcohol abuse. Treatment centers are also afraid that they cannot get jobs for older women. And jobs are considered a help to those who are trying to channel their free time into non-drinking lifestyles. On the other hand, those organizations that have senior citizens' apartments and group meal programs shudder at the thought of admitting an alcoholic into their midst. There is just no place for a woman senior citizen alcoholic.

The retirement colonies where so many old people put their life savings refuse to have an Alcoholics Anonymous group because it could "ruin" the name of the retirement settlement. Yet, the companionship of AA would in itself fill a need for these women who are drinking heavily because of loneliness. Rosin and Glatt in a study on geriatric alcoholism found that bereavement—with its loneliness and depression—and retirement—with its boredom, loss of status, and lowered income—were important elements in geriatric alcoholism. Sometimes all that the elderly need is to feel that someone is concerned about them. Once their depression lifts, they discover that they do not need alcohol in their lives.

Retirement colonies are often far away from stores, movies, and other facilities. Most retirement colonies permit only children over 18 if they permit anyone at all under 60 to live with a relative. In a sense, retirement colonies have broken up families and created an unnatural subculture.

THE DRINKING WOMAN: REVISITED

Many women who never drank before start when their husbands die. They may be shy about going out by themselves and, due to the lack of exercise and activities, may suffer from insomnia, which can frighten them. "Is old age doing this to me?" she'll ask her doctor. The doctor may prescribe her some pills making her feel something is truly wrong. She may decide that alcohol is her best companion, not realizing that it may annul or antagonize the function of the medicine she is taking. Drink makes some women feel they can recapture the sensation of youth and sometimes dull the sensation of ill health. If the elderly take alcohol to feel better, they will, unfortunately, only succeed in making themselves feel more depressed.

Old age may bring with it, too, the loss of wealth and status. For a career woman, the change can be harder than for a housewife. She may also have had a job which did not provide her with a pension. Many women were never trained for a job and, therefore, had low-paying jobs which did not permit them to save money. Others who were poor and single may have belonged to that generation in which a woman did not live alone but with relations. Now there may be no one for her to live with because she has out-lived those relations. If she is a widow, she may feel as useless as a retired career woman. Drink helps to bring back the good old memories. Old age for the lonely holds a pessimism about the future and evokes a desire to join a dead husband or parent. She may want to truly "drink herself to death."

We must not forget that alcoholism is a disease as much for the old as for the young. Older alcoholics deserve as much medical help and compassion as any group of people burdened with a disease.

The particular facts about alcohol, subculture, and cultural stress are as varied as the subcultures themselves. A social worker related how a group of older Slavic women living in Connecticut began for no visible reason to drink heavily. After getting to know them, she discovered that in their old country, the young people listened with respect to the older generation. Here in the United States, the young people not only didn't listen, but moved away and did what they wanted. The old women felt unneeded, non-respected, and misplaced.

Each culture has its peculiar stress. To understand the drinking woman it is important to look at the special stresses imposed upon her by her culture. Yet cultural stress must not be seen as simply negative. It can be good, too. It can make a culture grow. It can cause us to develop into better, stronger persons. Life is stress. As Hans Selye says, once stress ceases, life itself ceases.

Update
- Researchers emphasize that it was the European culture that introduced American Indians to alcohol. However, centuries ago the Aztecs' laws stated when and how much alcohol could be consumed. Permission to consume alcohol was determined by one's social status, role and age. Punishments for drinking infractions included death.
- Dr. Fred Beauvais, senior research scientist at the Tri-Ethnic Center for Prevention Research at Colorado State University reports, "—only one-third of the American Indian population" live on reservations, and yet, "most studies of drinking among American Indians have focused on Indians living on reservations or on traditional Indian land. —stereotype has perpetuated the image that all Indian people are afflicted with alcohol problems;—even scientific inquiry with its emphasis on problem definition has not focused on the vast numbers of Indian people who maintain sober and productive lives. (http://pubs.niaaa.nih.gov/publications/arh22-4/253.pdf)"
- John Hisnanick who is with the U.S. Census Bureau noted in 1992 that American Indian Reservations located in the southern parts of the United States have a lower rate of alcoholism than those located in the northern part of our country.
- Dr. Beauvais observed in various surveys that American Indian women had a 50% lower rate of alcoholism than American Indian men, as well as a lower rate of death from alcoholism.
- Dr. Beauvais reported (1992) that American Indian adolescent girls' rate of drinking is only slightly less than that of American Indian Boys.

- Both American Indian adults and youths tend to binge drink any available supply of alcohol until it is used up. (Dr. Philip May 1995)
- Because of the way we inherit the way we metabolize alcohol (See Updates at the end of Chapter 3 of this book) American Indians may be physically inclined to heavy drinking.
- Indian Health Services provide several regional treatment facilities for women.
- Some Alcoholics Anonymous groups incorporate American Indian traditions when meeting within proximity or on some American Indian territory.
- Dr. Philip May, one of whose many expertise is medical sociology, questions whether Indian reservations that don't permit drinking might not cause more problems, because those who drive off the reservation to drink will either be driving home while under the influence or may experience harm if they end up sleeping or passing out in an unsafe area.
- Older alcoholics may have special added health problems if drinking heavily. Most seniors take medicine that may interact poorly with alcohol.
- Seniors with a drinking problem may contribute to and/or worsen dementia and depression which is common among older adults.
- The elderly react more quickly to alcohol than the younger drinkers. Dr. Thomas P. Beresford along with Michael R. Lucey, Elizabeth M. Hill, James P. Young, Linda Demo-Dananberg after doing a study on 14 men and 14 women in the young (21–40 years) and 14 men and 15 women in the old (≥ 60 years) groups suggested that alcohol reacts faster in both the elderly men and women than in younger drinkers. Both elderly men and women who had been asked to fast and then were given alcohol showed higher average peak ethanol levels than gender-matched younger cohorts. It should be noted this effect was most pronounced in elderly women (47% vs 12%).

- A diagnostician may not realize if a senior manages to keep her drinking secret that the patient's pancreatitis, cirrhosis of the liver, cardiomyopathy, complaints of sleep problems, her falls and driving accidents are not due to age impairment but to her alcoholism. (Oslin 2004, SAMHSA 1998)

CHAPTER 11

LIFE WITH AN ALCOHOLIC

Before a husband, children, or a parent can reach out to help the woman alcoholic, the family has to take a good look at themselves and ask, "What has this woman's alcoholism done to us?" It doesn't matter whether they be rich or poor, black or white. Alcoholism, when it strikes, affects every family member.

A review of the material on the woman alcoholic and her effect on her family makes it clear that current knowledge is, to say the least, unsatisfactory. Most studies dwell on the male alcoholic, what his family suffers, and how the wife unknowingly and in desperation contributes to his drinking. This is unfair to the husband and children who live with an alcoholic woman. It makes them feel odd that they have a mother (and wife) who drinks. It makes the children and husband feel singled out. It makes them feel threatened. "What have we done to drive her to drink" is not an unusual question asked by her family.

The Father Worries

The turbulence alcoholism causes within a family touches every facet of their lives. While a man is at work, he can worry himself sick wondering if his drinking wife will forget to feed the baby. If she smokes, as so many alcoholics do, will she accidently burn a child when lighting a match? Will she pass out so that the little ones can't get into the house when the school bus drops them off? The father is so tense by the time he comes home that he can't contribute much of his true self to the children.

He may complain of lack of sleep. His thoughts at night may go something like this—"What business did she have insulting me unfairly in front of the children while she was drunk? O.K., she said those mean words only because she was drunk. But, what about all those broken promises? She promised me she wouldn't drink too much at our Thanksgiving dinner and embarrass me—but she broke her promise."

A little guilt may seep into his thoughts. "I yelled, maybe I acted too cold, and all that squabbling.... If I could just control myself!"

Nothing is right. He is afraid to bring his boss for dinner. He notices that the children also don't bring their friends home. He may be so busy trying to run the house that he may have dropped out of most community affairs. He may think, "I feel my friends look down on me for having an alcoholic wife." Many men have told their therapists, "Once I even asked my company to transfer me so we could have a new start."

Finance is a problem, too. He may say, "No matter how much I give her, it is lost. I have to tell the kids we better give up bowling this week. Their reaction is that I'm stingy. Then I lose my temper because I have taken all I can."

The Alcoholic Mother and Her Children

Children of the alcoholic are so disturbed by the drinking and arguing that some can't study. Others may walk out to stay at a friend's house without telling a parent where they are, or, in anger, will "take it out" on their friends, society, and teachers. Until the children realize that their mother is ill, they are afraid to talk about it to their friends, a knowing school counselor, or the family doctor. Often the family has trouble connecting their difficulties with a mother to a drinking problem.

Society heaps blame on the alcoholic mother and what she is doing to her children rather than on what the disease may cause her to do to her children. The damage, if unchecked by counseling, may be permanent. Her drinking makes her disgustingly dependent, rendering her vulnerable and causing her to avoid mothering responsibility.

The children lack a sense of security, love, and warmth so needed to develop the trust and confidence in themselves and others necessary for successful living. Many alcoholic mothers feel so guilty about their drinking that when they are not drinking, they try to make up for their drinking by pouring too much love on the child and thereby, nurture a clinging, dependent attitude in the child.

Since a mother spends more time with her children than a father, her problem can seriously affect the children. Her illness renders her impatient, quick to show her temper, unreasonable, demanding, extravagant. Some women act grandiose, "Listen children, I am going to buy each of you your own TV," and overly sentimental, "You know how my own daddy used to love me." Others act complainingly, "Your father is unfaithful to me." The children don't know whether the complaint is real or a figment of her inebriated imagination. She may become depressed or aggressive (throw things, hit the children) and pick quarrels. The children feel guilty. They think they must have done something wrong to incite their parent to drink. She may start a fire by dropping burning cigarettes, her staggering may break furniture, dishes. The children may feel they have to stay home for fear she may have a terrible accident, but are mortified to call anyone into the house. Unless they know how to cook and have money to shop, they may also go hungry. When little, the children are submissive. When adolescent, they rebel. They may stay out all night because, "I can't stand it at home." They may drink to impress their friends or to anesthetize their hurt and anger. They may let out their hostilities in the form of aggressive acts against people and property. Boys tend to rebel against property; girls rebel by acting out in the area of sex. A boy or girl who feels ashamed of her home may feel rejected by peers and social groups. Such youngsters may choose to follow a unique religion, be critical and punitive, act respectively ultra-feminine or masculine, and flirt, but feel, deep down, an emptiness. These children may not know how to cope with every day problems because the only example of coping they saw at home was to "take a drink."

When To Tell a Woman She Is Ill

The hangover can be a moment of truth for the family and the alcoholic. If the children remind her of her grandiose promises ("Each one of you will have your own TV"), she will deny having ever said it. She truly does not remember because her alcoholism causes lapses of memory known as blackouts. She will be physically ill, dizzy, weak, drained, have a pounding head and frequently feel nauseous. She may tremble and suffer tremendous fear and anxiety. She will feel guilty remorse toward her family and be angry with herself. It is usually at this point that the family of the alcoholic can tell her that alcoholism is a disease, that she is truly ill, that the illness is not a disgrace and can be treated. Many an alcoholic has, at such moments talked to an Alcoholics Anonymous member, her minister, the family doctor, or, because she feels so desperately ill, willingly entered a treatment facility or a hospital. A child saying, "Mommy, I missed you while you drank," may motivate her to do something about her drinking. Deep down, she knows that her loud hostilities or angry silences hang way out when she drinks. One day that same sweet child talking may have had enough and might run away or cause some other family crisis.

It is best for the family to talk in terms of their love for her, how they worry about her and how they would like her to go for help for "her problem." A phrase like "your problem" makes more sense to her than a "stop drinking" command because, aside from medical discomfort, she has the problem of despair and of deep unhappiness.

If the alcoholic refuses to listen to the family, they should try to get someone outside of the family to talk to her. The alcoholic is so used to the family's nagging that she may not listen anymore. A doctor can give her an unbiased medical diagnosis. A clergyman may tell her about other people in the community who live as arrested alcoholics.

The Family of the Alcoholic as the Unit Needing Help

It is not enough for the alcoholic to seek relief. Fifty percent of her progress depends on the willingness of her husband and family to seek help as well. The family may at first not recognize that the drinking has any effect on them. The children and her husband may have taken seriously her insults and profound silences.

When a mother and wife has negated her responsibility, the family roles get switched about. The daughter may clean and cook. The son may hold an after-school job to earn money for food which she spent for liquor. The family under such circumstances is more anxious than the alcoholic. This anxiety within the family causes the alcoholic, even if she did stay off the alcohol for a while, to seek relief in the bottle from "this mad" family.

The Single Alcoholic Woman and Her Family

Amidst the growing awareness of the problems of the drinking woman and her family, the special problems of the single woman alcoholic living with her parents have not received the attention they deserve.

Roles may get switched about when a grown daughter who is an alcoholic lives at home like a "baby." The unmarried daughter living at home should be worrying about her parents' health as the parents grow older, and not the parents about their grown daughter. The parents should be busy with their own activities, trips, and friends. Instead, mother may still make her bed for her. Daddy may give her an allowance and pay for golf lessons. All the while, her parents may be scolding her that she did not achieve adulthood as all her other girl friends did.

The parents may be prisoners of their attitudes. They may be "parenting" her too much when they should have let her grow up years ago. Perhaps they did not give her enough parenting when she was young, and she is still looking for "mommy to nurse me." Or, is their daughter copying a parent's drinking pattern? Certainly, the parents can't lead a full and happy life with such a problem in their home. Deep down, they wonder, "What did we do to contribute to our daughter's drinking?" Such parents should seek counseling themselves and should encourage their daughter to enter a live-in treatment center until she is well. If she is old enough, she should be held responsible for her own actions which would include her moving into her own living quarters and earning her own livelihood.

In one treatment center, the single women were not permitted to phone their parents until they had completed a three-month stay in the center. During the second three months they were advised to phone their parents only once a week. The reason some treatment centers are so strict is that the parents of such a daughter may have interfered too much when their daughter made a decision.

When she leaves the treatment center, unless she is completely recovered, her parents can undo all the good. Father may interfere when she decides to date again. The parents may discourage her from taking her own apartment and building up her own career. They may infantalize her. If the parents were critical of her or cold to her while she was growing up, they may revert to the same interaction once she lives at home. Their daughter has to understand why they behave like this so that she can cope once she is out of the treatment center.

There was a case of a 35-year-old woman in a treatment center who had never chosen her own clothes. The center considered it progress when the woman went out alone to buy some clothes; That same day her mother came to visit and told her daughter to return the clothes because they looked awful. The center convinced the daughter not to see the mother again until her mother also went into therapy, or she, the daughter, was healthier.

The Family of the Alcoholic

In order for a family to help themselves, the members have to make the alcoholic daughter or mother/wife responsible for her own drinking and, whenever possible, for the household. Whether she is a divorced woman living with "mommy and daddy," or a single girl still at home, or a married mother and wife; it is time to let her come back as a responsible member of the family. This may be harder for the family than they realize.

When the Mother Comes Back Home

If the alcoholic woman lives with husband and children, the children are used to making their own decisions and taking care of their sick mother. As the mother tries to resume her role, she may hear, "What do you mean I should come in at 11 P.M.—I am used to staying out as late as I please." The father may say, "I always give the children money for food—the last time I gave you money, you drank it all up!" The youngest may cry, when hurt, for the older sister because "Mommy frightens me." If she is away from home and if she can't care for her children while in treatment or has induced problems in them, her guilt and self-contempt may be intensified. Unless the family cooperates, she will not feel needed.

Making the Alcoholic Responsible

When a woman decides to drink, it is, in the end, her responsibility. Treating a woman like a child by protecting her reputation, hiding the liquor or pouring it out of the bottle takes the responsibility away from her. When she drinks, the family does not have to sit by and watch.

One girl told her therapist how, when her mother drank, each family member got stomach cramps because she used to let all her self-hate out on them. One day the family told the mother that they love her when she is sober, but they really did not want to stay around while she drank. The alcoholic mother threatened them with, "I'll take the next bus out of town." The family answered, "We'll miss you, but that is completely your decision and choice." The next time she drank the whole family went out to the movies. She did eventually stop drinking.

A family can very rarely act so resolutely on its own. It needs an objective outside supportive source such as Al-Anon, Alateen, and/or family therapy. It cannot be emphasized enough how important it is for those who live with an alcoholic to seek help. Indirectly, they will help the alcoholic, too.

Family Service

Most towns in the United States have family service and/or Mental Health or United Community Service. These agencies cater to a community's needs. They have information on alcoholism. They know what families will take teenagers as guests so they may cool off from their family problems. Others arrange day care centers. Many offer family therapy.

Hot Lines

Many towns have hot lines, which is a telephone number where any member of the community can call for information about the various facilities. The person answering the phone may help the caller to work out his anger and focus his problems. Names of the callers are never asked.

National Runaway Safe Line

Youngsters may phone National Runaway Safe Line, dial (800)-786-2929. A counselor at the other end helps to identify the problem together with the caller. "I am angry because—", "I am leaving home because—." The agency will tell the youngster where to go for help in his or her town. If the youngster has run away and wants to get a message to the parents without revealing where she or he is, the agency will arrange a conference call keeping his confidentiality. An upset mother or father is as welcome to phone them confidentially as a youngster.

Family Counseling

Sometimes families are afraid to enter family counseling because each member may think "this is all my fault." Therapy does exactly the opposite. The therapist is usually someone with whom the family feels they have something in common. The therapist may also have a family and be of the same ethnic background. Rapport and partnership is established with the therapist after a few sessions. The therapist takes away the sting of blame and punishment in a family. The therapist defines the misunderstandings, confessions, and distortions in a family by pointing out what is really wrong. The son may be angry that he has to have that after-school job and had to give up being on the varsity team. The father may call the daughter lazy when she does, in reality, not know how to cook anything but spaghetti and hamburgers. Once everyone airs their views, there come new avenues of action and alignment in the family. The therapist also makes the alcoholic responsible for her actions and takes the blame and the guilt away from the family. He will give her the courage to face up to her financial, family, legal, and medical problems. She herself may have ignored her religious and vocational needs. It was easier to anesthetize her central nervous system with alcohol than face her talents. The family, as well as she, has to think what was painful for her. She has to learn problem-solving techniques that do not include alcohol. While in treatment, the therapist may point out to the husband how he is emphasizing his wife's dependent role instead of encouraging her to be independent.

The alcoholic may try to avoid responsibility and gain sympathy by having a hundred and one excuses. She may in essence say, "Please, I am just a helpless thing." She may justify her need to be helpless by saying, "I was very bright (self-justification combined with superiority), but I dropped out of college so there would be tuition money for my younger brother." While in treatment, she may avoid positive action by wavering back to helplessness and inadequacy. "My teachers said I would have made an excellent biologist, but now, of course, it is too late." Is it too late? An objective person as a therapist can point out to her, her questionable thinking. If the family tries to talk to her, she might tell them off!

The family can nevertheless be supportive. A supportive family is one who lets her know what she is worth to them.

The therapist may make the family aware that their non-supportive behavior may be due to the fact that her past pattern of drinking may keep the family from thinking that it may be any different next week. "She always drinks when Dad goes on a business trip" may be the comment of her children. The therapist may encourage the children to think, "When Dad's on a business trip, we'll do the dishes so Mom can get out every night in time for her AA meeting." Such thinking helps to realign a child's image of the self and of the family.

The therapist will try to shift the bad feelings within a family. Is the husband holding back some of his affection and pleasure because he is too concerned with fortifying his authority and discipline? Is sharing sacrificed so that the husband can work all the time? Are there unhealthy alignments in the family such as dad and daughter against mother? Or mother and daughter against father? Is there a trouble maker in the family? The trouble maker may be the weak one in the family upon whom everyone lets their troubles out. This so-called scapegoat will in some way retaliate, hence, the "trouble maker." When the mother stops drinking, the family may seek a new scapegoat to continue their habitual patterns of criticizing and picking on a family member.

The therapist's encouragement to interact, to give warmth, rubs off on the family. He notes that family life is the training ground for getting along with other people. He may at times note what the family avoids talking about. For example, "My son who looks just like my brother the trouble maker is no good." They avoid facing the fact that he was never accepted for his real worth, but judged by his looks.

The parents when alone with the therapist may try to avoid discussing sex. The therapist serves as a reality tester. The wife may say, "Every time my husband works late, I drink because I feel that he is having an affair." Is he truly having an affair or does the alcoholic have such a low opinion of herself that she cannot think otherwise? Other sexual problems may reveal themselves. The husband may not stimulate his wife sufficiently so that she does not experience an orgasm. A woman may feel it is her fault and drink because she feels she is a sexual failure. Of course, the consequences of too much drinking makes her look neglected, less womanly, and aggravate the very feelings of doubts she already has. All these problems are solvable.

Some family problems such as drinking may reach as far back as three or four generations. It is the emotional influence of their present family life that may evoke some of these problems. The therapist explores the day-to-day difficulties in a family while researching with the family, the origin of these conflicts. This is very important because children unconsciously copy their parents and such family research (some therapists even draw "family trees" to emphasize their family origins) may keep them from using alcohol and all other drugs when confronted with stress. Just hearing their mother say "how" she started to drink and "why" she drank opens up an avenue of compassion for Mom. From this shift of feelings may come new strength and healthy alliances of family members.

Alateen and Al-Anon

Other invaluable groups which families attend, sometimes in conjunction with family therapy, are Alateen and Al-Anon. Some families' needs are so fulfilled by these two groups that they find they need no other agency to help them. Al-Anon is a self-help group for adults and Alateen is a self-help group for teenagers only.

Both have developed out of Alcoholics Anonymous, a self-help group for alcoholics. Their purpose is to help those living with an alcoholic to regain their strength and stability.

Alateen

Teenagers who have an alcoholic parent have said that Alateen changed their whole lives. In Alateen, they can talk to other teenagers who also have an alcoholic parent. Alateens encourage one another and learn effective ways to cope with their problems. Alateens air out their problems of living with an alcoholic. Each member realizes that other teenager's too have moments where it is difficult for them to act appropriately toward their ill parent. In talking to these teenager's, one will find that one's own personal experiences can help them, too.

In all discussions, last names are never mentioned and specific personal acts are never described. The sponsor of each Alateen group who is an Alcoholics Anonymous member, Al-Anon member, or an understanding experienced Alateen member, helps lead the discussions. Alateens will on occasion have parents come from Alcoholics Anonymous to tell them what they went through before they arrested their drinking. This is always a marvelous opportunity to ask questions.

Teenagers who belong to Alateen never feel alone. They make friends among themselves. When they visit each other, no one has to "explain" why a parent in the home is ill. In between group meetings when things are rough at home, those teen-agers can phone the group's sponsor or a fellow member who will discuss the immediate problem with them without interfering in the parent's way of life. For example, if a member has a geometry exam to cram for, and one of his parents is drinking, an experienced Alateen member will not tell the parent to stop drinking, but will concern himself with his fellow member. If he is upset, a fellow Alateen member might calm him by reminding him that his parent is ill and that his parent has to come to his own decision to do something about his drinking. If necessary, he will get the teenager out of the house to help her to find a peaceful place to study, be it the library or another member's home. Should a teenager find his situation at home intolerable because a parent is abusive, a fellow Alateen member may on occasion offer his home until the parent sobers up.

Alateens are, when necessary, also members of Alcoholics Anonymous. Drinking may on rare occasions start as young as age ten. Junior high school and high school youngsters who want to experiment with drugs say alcohol is cheaper than dope, easily obtainable, often found at home, and legally retailed. For some, it is a passing phase. Some unfortunately, become alcoholics. Alateens have learned the symptoms of alcoholism, and, those that drink are able to catch themselves in the early stage of the illness. They are aware that having a parent who is an alcoholic, they come from a "high risk" family. Many Alateens drink socially once they reach the legal drinking age, and never become alcoholics.

Al-Anon

Al-Anon works on the same principles as Alateen and Alcoholics Anonymous. Mothers and fathers discuss in part how to better their relationships with their children, how to have greater compassion for their sons' and daughters' experiences with alcoholism, and how to help the alcoholic realize that she is ill. Quite often when an alcoholic single woman or a mother sees her family pull themselves together and treat her with the knowledge that her compulsive drinking is a sickness, she herself may be motivated to seek help.

The vast majority of Al-Anon members are women. However, Al-Anon has noted more and more men joining the fellowship. Many Al-Anon groups have organized stag groups where the men may feel freer to discuss their doubts and problems. Al-Anon in its brochure, "What's Next? Asks the Husband of the Alcoholic," says "Pride does peculiar things. As men (the stronger sex, remember?), we are not likely to admit that a mere woman has presented us with a problem we can't handle." Al-Anon counsels, "For years you have probably been asking yourself, 'Why did this happen to me?' Now that you know how sick she is, try asking, 'Why did this happen to her?'"

Al-Anon helps the husband to preserve his own well-being, to sort out his problem from her problems. Is it really her fault that her husband did not get the promotion? Are we using her drinking as a scapegoat for all our problems? Or is it only a convenient excuse? Just as the alcoholic has to learn about her illness, what it does to her and her family, so the husband has to learn what alcoholism has done to him, to their marriage, and to his personality. It may come as a surprise to him that most drinkers try to implicate the people they love only as a means of justifying their drinking. He may also be amazed to learn that husbands, whether they do it consciously or unconsciously, determine in many ways a wife's drinking behavior.

Al-Anon is listed in the local telephone books. They also have all the information about the Alateen meetings. One may write directly to 1600 Corporate Landing Pkwy, Virginia Beach, VA 23454 (757)-563-1600 The main office will gladly mail pamphlets and news of the nearest branches.

Live-in Treatment Centers

A new and much needed facility for men, women and children living with an alcoholic are the residential treatment centers for families. You may find information at www.helpguide.org/mental/choosing_alcohol_rehab_treatment.htm or at 1-(800)-604-0025.

Some centers have out-patient clinics where men may be treated too. One of these centers, Rainbow Retreat in Arizona (no longer available), says they have found some of the men to be the nurturing, rigid type who "need" a helpless (drinking) woman. Once the men are aware of their own behavior and what makes them behave as the nurturing rigid type, the treatment is usually fruitful.

There are indications that treatment centers geared to help those who have been battered physically and mentally are growing. Of course, one thinks more of the poor "black and blue" wife of the alcoholic husband needing shelter than of a husband of the alcoholic wife needing a home. He nevertheless does need treatment as much as any other member living within an alcoholic family.

Hopefully, all husbands, parents, and children living with an alcoholic will get in touch with one of these many services. Remember, you are not alone. There are at least 40 million people in our country affected by someone else's drinking.

Updates
- Don't have an Al-anon or an Alateen group near you—visit them on line at www.al-anon.alateen.org/electronic-meetings.
- Youngsters in danger because they are living with an alcoholic mother who is not coping should phone The Bureau For At-Risk Youth 1-(800)-99-YOUTH or get in touch with Child Abuse Hotline (800)-422-4453.
- Youngsters living with a drinking Mom are sometimes in danger of an inappropriate boyfriend visiting the home. RAIN (national network for rape, abuse, incest victims) can be reached at (800)-656-4673.
- Children who have a Mom who drinks too much can reach out to National Association For Children of Alcoholics (www.nacoa.org) at (888)-554-COAS and/or get in touch with National Boys Town Line (also for girls) (800)-448-3000.
- In the book, *For Teenagers Living With A Parent Who Abuses Alcohol/Drugs*, the author suggests on page 128, that family members living with an alcoholic, no matter whether a child or an adult, join on line IN THE ROOMS (http://www.intherooms.com). "There are over 240,000 members who are willing to share their experience, strength and hope with you. Everyone is anonymous". Alcoholics as well will find appropriate fellowships on this site. Once on the site pick the group you feel is for you."
- What does a family history of drinking do to the next generation? Visit www.adultchildren.org for help.
- American Natives living with an alcoholic who want to seek help from their own physicians can contact www.aaip.com, the Association of American Indian Physicians. Be sure to click on health and information resources.

CHAPTER 12

ALCOHOLICS ANONYMOUS

There are many places an alcoholic can seek help, but the most renowned of all the treatments for alcoholics is probably Alcoholics Anonymous. AA works so well that most of the halfway houses, detoxification centers, hospitals, treatment centers, rehabilitation centers, and other recovery facilities invite AA to set up meetings for their patients. Many AA's meet in churches and synagogues not because AA is a religious organization but simply because space is available. According to its own statistics AA has 16,000 groups throughout the USA and 292,000 members.

AA is a group of alcoholics who help each other to gain and maintain sobriety. The AA program includes "12 Suggested Steps" to help the alcoholic maintain sobriety. The first step, which many consider the most important step, is the recognition by the alcoholic that she is powerless over alcohol. At each meeting, one step is discussed thoroughly and a member tells "her" story to the group. By sharing, he or she helps the others to come to grips with their drinking.

AA has many publications which are either free to the public or which cost very little. These publications emphasize mostly the AA program of recovery. One describes AA as "a world-wide fellowship of men and women who help each other to maintain sobriety and who offer to share their recovery experience freely with others who may have a drinking problem."

Alcoholics Anonymous in Your Community, distributed by AA publications, says that AA is a "method of treating alcoholism in which members act as therapists to each other sharing with each other a large body of similar experiences in suffering and recovering from alcoholism." Some of the pamphlets are done in very realistic comic book style. "It Happened to Alice," depicting a woman alcoholic, is especially good.

The group experience in AA helps each alcoholic to realize that she can help others as others help her. AA helps her to resocialize. Each new member who wants to stop drinking is introduced to a sponsor, also an alcoholic, and usually a fellow woman.

What most impresses the new member about her sponsor is that she looks healthy, is well-dressed and full of pep, and has zest for life. The alcoholic should be able to phone her sponsor whenever she thinks she cannot control her drinking. The sponsor should be as helpful at two o'clock in the morning as two o'clock in the afternoon. If the sponsor does not live up to these ideals, the new AA cohort should have the courage to ask for someone else to act as a sponsor. Ideally, the sponsor understands the good, and the bad moods, the slips, the tears, the humiliations, and the aches because she has been through it all herself.

Some sponsors broaden their education on alcoholism beyond their own experience by taking courses on alcoholism sponsored by their local hospitals and universities. Some of these sponsors go on to earn a degree and take paid jobs as counselors in the field of alcoholism in the various treatment centers, clinics, and hospitals. We will meet some of these ladies in our Seeking Help chapter. Within AA, however, sponsors are never paid.

Women and AA

In the very beginning, some women feel shy at any AA meeting. Members, whether men or women, try to make a new member feel comfortable. After all, they have all been through it themselves and know that frightened feeling of being new. This shyness may at times affect women more so than men. This may be particularly true if there are only one or two other women in the group. As one woman puts it, "Men have so many more relevant histories to relate than I would. A man will say, 'Whenever I made a sale, I celebrated it in a bar.' People understand that. All I could say was, 'When my washing machine broke down, I drank.' Can anybody understand that?"

Another woman said she was silent at AA meetings because she was fascinated by what the men revealed. Never would a husband or a boyfriend talk in private so intimately (regardless of whether he is an alcoholic or has no problem with drinking) about his pressures, his feelings, and his actions.

Perhaps women have been brainwashed by teenage and women's magazines to be "good listeners because you'll be popular with the boys."

The question is, too, whether occasionally a man in the group may not demonstrate a subtle disgust with women alcoholics more than with his male cohorts because he just doesn't like to see a woman drink. This is an individual problem that could surface in any group, be it a hospital, family, or in a club.

Many men accept women alcoholics intellectually but not emotionally. A man who seeks to prove his masculinity by drinking may arrest his drinking in AA but still not change his attitude toward women who enter the male domain of drinking.

Some women do feel it is worse for her to drink than it is for a man. She may have gotten this feeling in very subtle ways. She may have heard her neighbors chide—"How could she do this to her family?" She may have heard the same people refer to a drinking man as someone who was "driven to drink." She may have been hauled before a judge for drunken driving, who, in sympathy to the family, dismissed the case. This only succeeded in making her feel that alcoholism, the disease, is an unmentionable defect.

One woman in AA pointed out, "In most AA's, it is the women who make coffee; the women are the secretaries. There is a male clubbish feeling in too many AA groups. Not all men, but many, still have their bar-style attitude toward women, and will now pick a woman up at AA instead of the old bar." The author would like to add that many women told her that they like to meet men at AA because these men understand what they went through. Some men and women at AA date each other. It is wonderful not having to explain why they are not having a cocktail before a meal in an elegant restaurant. Some are wise and realize that they have to work out each of their problems before they would want a binding relationship. A few do tie the knot and end up often happily married to each other.

Many women say AA reflects the community where it holds its meetings. An AA lunch meeting in the heart of Wall Street in New York City would be entirely different than a meeting held in a small suburban bedroom town where perhaps it is not as prevalent for a woman to work. The woman in the small suburban bedroom town is probably as content at her AA meeting as the woman working in Wall Street is at hers.

Some AA groups offer in conjunction with their regular meeting, a once-a-week regular closed meeting for women only. At closed meetings for "women only," women open up. The lone woman drinker can be reached more easily in a woman's meeting.

Women Only Groups

The women only groups tend to become very intimate and discuss issues only indirectly related to alcoholism. It is here that the drinking woman will talk about the hurt of her husband's infidelities, and her worries about her children. She will talk about her vanities—and they do hurt—how when intoxicated she lost control of her bladder in public, how she collapsed at her children's birthday party, how she realized she was shaking so that she was putting her makeup on crookedly but still insisted on putting it on to go out to the PTA meeting. She may talk about her parents. How she never realized that one of them was a heavy drinker. Or, that she had been too young when she had lost a parent through death, divorce, mental illness, alcoholism, or abandonment and therefore, never had the chance to build up the emotional security she needed. She may talk about how a parent was not kind to her, demanded too much of her or was never satisfied. She may talk about her poor image of herself.

The "women only" meeting may also be particularly important to the single woman who is a lone drinker. Single women usually have difficulty establishing relations with men. The older female members in AA (also in co-ed groups) give her the confidence and sometimes the mothering she may need. Since such women may come from homes where the parents may have discouraged any dating or going out with peer group friends, they are very dependent upon a "parent" type. These women may have started to drink when their parent died because they were lonely and depressed and still needed a parent. Some may have started to drink when they did date and needed confidence.

Whether a woman is in a co-ed or all-female AA group, in AA a woman comes out of her isolation, boredom, and feelings of powerlessness. AA teaches that success is a day-by-day process. AA helps to transfer dependencies to constructive outlets such as helping other people. Until the alcoholic comes to terms with her drinking, she may fool herself and turn to another addiction. It is said that only when we can relate to our cohorts' stories in AA are we in touch with our drinking. In AA, women learn to talk and to make friends.

Joyce's Story
Let's meet one of the AA ladies who told how she was introduced to AA.

When Joyce went to her doctor for her yearly checkup, he asked her how much she drank. She didn't know whether her family had told him that she drank too much or whether he had noticed something during her examination. Joyce told her doctor that she went for days without alcohol, but, she admitted reluctantly, that when she drank, she could not remember the next day how much she had had. Her doctor told her he thought that she was an alcoholic, and he would like her to go to AA. He asked her if she would follow through on his medical instructions. Joyce knew she wouldn't, but she didn't dare say "No" to him so she promised her doctor she would go to AA. However, she told him she had lost her driver's license due to her drinking. He told her that Kay W., who lived three houses down from her, would be glad to give her a lift in her car. Joyce couldn't believe that Kay, who always seemed so active, so well, so efficient, could be an alcoholic. The next day, Kay had made arrangements to take Joyce that same evening to an AA meeting. Joyce was so frightened at the thought of having to become "as good as Kay" that she drank heavily all day and passed out. Joyce's daughter had no choice but to phone Kay and tell her that her mother was sick. Kay invited Joyce's daughter to come to AA with her.

Joyce's daughter said, "What, and leave Mom?"

"Why not?" Kay countered. "She's a big girl and it's time you let her be responsible for her own actions."

Joyce's daughter left her mother a note saying that she had gone to an open AA meeting and would bring Kay back with her after the meeting.

When Joyce woke up and saw her daughter's note, she was furious. How dare Kay stop by and see her in this condition? And to make matters worse, she would probably give her a righteous lecture. When Kay arrived with Joyce's daughter from the AA meeting, Kay asked if there was anything she could do to help. Kay told Joyce that she had done the same thing, drunk herself sick the first time she was supposed to go to AA. When she finally did go to AA, she had about three more slips until she admitted to herself that she was an alcoholic. Kay left Joyce some pamphlets about AA and told her that she would like to invite her the next day to a breakfast AA meeting where they would serve coffee and donuts. She also told Joyce that it would be a particularly good meeting for her because it was a "beginner's meeting," which means all the others would be at the same stage as Joyce. Joyce felt much more relaxed when Kay left because she knew no one expected her to be perfect at AA. She felt something that she had not felt for years: a glimmer of hope that she might be at the threshold of a new life.

The nearest AA is listed in all phone books or one can write to: Alcoholics Anonymous, Box 459, Grand Central P.O., New York, N.Y. 10017.

Intergroups

Each county or area has its own AA intergroup. Intergroups are established to carry out certain functions common to all the groups in that particular area. They list the day and time and location of each meeting available in the area. The list includes the closed meetings for women. For example, one small town in suburbia of New York City has as many as ten different groups which average cumulatively six different meetings per day. One can go during lunch, before work, or after work. Some are for both men and women, others are for men only or for women only. Other meetings are for beginners. Beginners' meetings are like all the other meetings except the members being new feel more comfortable with each other. Some women go to two meetings, which may include a "for women only" as well as a "for men and women" meeting. Some alcoholics go, in the beginning when it is hard to give up drinking, to two or three meetings a day. Others may go once a day or once a week as their need may be.

Some inter groups have a hospital referral desk. The attendant is glad to suggest the most appropriate facilitiy for each patient's needs. It is important to know which hospitals will take alcoholics. Unfortunately, there are still hospitals who look upon an alcoholic as someone they would rather ignore. AA and its members will have this valuable information.

Although officially it is not mentioned, AA members always seem to know of jobs available for those who may need one. They have the addresses of the best baby-sitters in town, and the right doctors or therapists. They are an invaluable and resourceful group. They are so successful that other people who have problems with "over-eating" or "chain smoking" have tried to overcome their problems by copying their method.

There is only one Alcoholics Anonymous and those alcoholics who stick with it, who put up with the first few hard weeks or months, find the reward beyond anything they have ever experienced.

Unfortunately, there are not enough AA's throughout the nation. The 16,000 groups are too few for the 9 million estimated alcoholics in the U.S.

Furthermore, many women do not diagnose themselves as alcoholics and thus are dependent on their family doctor to diagnose the illness. Others are so sick that they need sleep-in facilities.

And perhaps worst of all, many who have been deserted by their families know that they are sick, but are so discouraged, so down and out, that they do not know how to pick up the pieces.

For these women, too, there is hope. Much hope.

Updates
- If you have transportation difficulties or are not feeling well you can participate with an AA group on line. Go to www.aa-intergroup.org
- Visit http://www.agnosticaanyc.org/worldwide.html to find an Agnostic or Atheist AA meeting.
- AA cooperates with legal professionals, courts, clergies, businesses, all types of correctional facilities, grass roots organizations, and individual ethnic groups to inaugurate the needed AA groups.
- 35% of AA members in the United States and Canada are women according to a 2011 survey.
- Women Alcoholics Anonymous members for the past 50 years have been arranging annual conferences to share experiences common to women alcoholics, discuss problems particular to women AA members and to have the opportunity to hear AA women speakers from all over the country. For more information visit http://www.internationalwomensconference.org
- To find a list of AA meetings catering to gay gals go to gal-aa.org
- The Terman Study (The Terman objective is explained in this book at the end of Chapter 6 under the Updates heading) revealed that religious women lived longer. It was not the praying or the meditation that enhanced women's longevity rather the community life, helping others, the ties to other people. If you don't belong to a church or synagogue AA gives you that same sense of helping new comers, making friends, receiving compassion, connecting with others at the end of meetings for coffee, and joining them on weekends in non-alcoholic activities such as picnics, going to the movies or gathering for a non-alcoholic dinner out.

CHAPTER 13

SEEKING HELP

There are a great many avenues of approach to the treatment of alcoholism. There are treatment centers, detoxification clinics, halfway houses, doctors specializing in the field, and counselors ready to help her readjust to society. Unfortunately, some women when groping for help from their clergy, family, or friends, still are treated with: "For Heaven's sake, pull yourself together; you shame the family." This is an impossible assignment for an alcoholic who has lost control. How clergy, friends, doctors, and counselors in the treatment center approach the patient can bolster self-esteem and thus improve chances for recovery. Seeking help is a delicate matter, and involves evaluating not only the type of facilities available but the approach used by the helping profession.

Doctors

There are many doctors who diagnose alcoholism and treat it correctly. But in order to avoid medical pitfalls, it is important to look closely at those doctors who are not comfortable with the thought of a female alcoholic sitting in their offices.

Many a woman has tried to broach in a round about way the subject of alcoholism with her doctor—be he a psychiatrist, family doctor, internist, or a bone specialist fixing her broken leg by telling him her troubles in managing the home and coping with her family. Many doctors retreat from the real problem of a woman alcoholic and blame her complaints on her biological background and prescribe medicine for her aches and pains. He'll treat her with valium or librium or barbituates. Many women will stop drinking for a while and become "pill intoxicants." It is more ladylike to take prescribed drugs because it is associated with a respectable profession and escapes detection. Prescribing drugs to an alcoholic can be dangerous; she may disregard the doctor's orders and take a week's supply all in one gulp. She always figures out a way to get more drugs. She may get prescriptions from several doctors at once, each thinking only he is prescribing for the patient.

Many people think that sedatives are not addictive. Once addicted, however, patients report that when they are withdrawing, they feel grouchy, irritable and/ or have difficulty sleeping.

Other doctors will tell their patient, "You are an alcoholic," and let it go at that. Yet doctors should be able to prescribe proper treatment for a patient. There are, aside from Alcoholics Anonymous, internists and psychiatrists or outpatient clinics all specializing in alcoholism. A family doctor should know which type or combination of treatment is best for his patient. He himself may not necessarily be trained to treat an alcoholic, but he should know to whom he can send her just as he knows to whom to send a patient with an eye infection.

The study of alcoholism is still a pioneer field in all areas of medicines, especially psychiatry. Psychiatrists specializing in alcoholism are needed in helping the alcoholic to regain her emotional equilibrium and to see what it was that caused her to become addicted. For example, it is not uncommon for a psychiatrist to treat a patient for depression without realizing that the patient was using alcohol all the time to relieve her symptoms. Once the psychiatrist discovers this, he may feel he can no longer work with such a patient. In order for a psychiatrist to succeed in treating an alcoholic, he must inspect his own feelings about this disease. Dr. A. N. Browne-Mayers, Associate Medical Director, National Council on Alcoholism, says, "There is no such thing as a hopeless patient. There are only lazy psychiatrists.

"Psychiatrists don't like to be lied to. They like to feel that they have the complete confidence of the patient while they are working out a problem together with their patient. An alcoholic, until she admits to herself that she is an alcoholic, will deny her alcoholism. If necessary, she will lie about her drinking. 'You see, doctor, I missed my appointment with you because my youngest daughter needed me at home, and I just forgot to cancel my appointment. It can happen to anybody.' However, if the doctor shows his confidence in his patient, she will eventually say, 'You know all those appointments I missed—I was really drunk.'"

Many positive and encouraging developments have occurred in the American medical field that promise help to all alcoholics. As a result of a recent decision by the National Board of Medical Examiners, questions relating to alcoholism will be included on the medical licensing examinations which are used by all states. That means no future medical doctor will be able to practice without knowledge of the disease, alcoholism. The examination questions will be submitted each year by the National Council on Alcoholism. We can expect that the new requirement will encourage all medical schools to include "America's most neglected disease" in their medical school curricula.

This should provide a marked improvement in the medical care available to the drinking woman. It should mean that our family doctors as well as those doctors specializing in the field of women, such as obstetricians and gynecologists, will be able to recognize at an early stage the symptoms of alcoholism. It will mean that the doctor will be able to explain to the patient and the family in lucid terms and without making them feel they are a disgrace or "different," what alcoholism is and what treatment he recommends. This is particularly important because alcoholics often feel weak compared to those who are able to drink socially. By his attitudes a doctor may inadvertently reinforce this feeling, especially if he himself is a heavy drinker who has convinced himself that he, as a doctor, is above such a problem.

Emergency Ward

The alcoholic woman is not a stranger in the emergency ward of her local hospital. Many a medical student's first patient was an alcoholic with a broken leg, burns, or a concussion from an automobile accident. Doctors in an emergency ward up to now have said they don't have time to start talking about alcoholism, and some hospitals haven't accepted a diagnosis of alcoholism on a chart. The doctors may talk among themselves about the patient's "ethanolism," or speak about her as someone "who drinks more than I do." A male doctor may find it inconvenient to confront a woman patient with her alcoholism, particularly if he has then to tell her children, who may be grown, or her husband, who may want her out of the hospital as soon as possible.

Hopefully, future doctors may finally realize the importance of putting this disease on a medical chart when an inebriated patient is brought into the emergency following an alcohol-induced accident.

Additional Resources

Realistically speaking, the additional resources that may be available today to a woman depends on where one lives. At the present moment, the Federal Government is embarking on supporting many programs on a statewide and community level, The Veterans Administration Hospitals have alcoholism programs for both men and women. Many state hospitals also have their own alcoholism programs which reach out into the community. In addition, private hospitals and volunteer hospitals all over the country have clinics with alcoholism programs oriented to their own communities.

There are many ways of finding out what treatment facilities may be near you. Your doctor may well know of one. If your doctor is similar to the ones we described a few pages ago and who says, "It is not so serious and perhaps you should try some valium," you should not be too bashful to discuss with him his reasons for giving you valium. He may have perfectly good reasons for prescribing this particular drug. However, if you cannot comfortably communicate with him, you perhaps should seek another doctor. Your mental health service and your library are good resources for finding help. The National Council on Alcoholism (today known as National Council on Alcoholism and Drug Dependence NCADD), a national voluntary health agency which was founded to combat the disease of alcoholism, has "Alcoholism Information Centers" listed in the telephone books throughout the United States or at www.recovery.org. N.C.A. was founded in 1943 by Marty Mann, a woman, with the help of the Yale Center on Alcohol Studies. An alcoholic herself, she became concerned with educating the public about alcohol and alcoholism. The Council encourages and has a support program for research on alcoholism. Should there not be such a center near you, you can write to National Council on Alcoholism and Drug Dependence, 217 Broadway, Suite 712, New York, NY 10007, phone: 212.269.7797, fax:212.269.7510, www.ncadd.org.

Other centers ready to help are:
- The National Institute on Alcohol Abuse and Alcoholism or NIAAA), with the aid of federal funds, has put out an Alcoholism Treatment Facilities Directory covering all of the in—and out-patient facilities in the United States and Canada. This directory is also available by individual states. They can be reached at http://www.niaaa.nih.gov/ or telephone (301)-443-2594 or CRAN@mail.nih.gov;
- American Society of Addiction Medicine, 4601 North Park Avenue, Upper Arcade, Suite 101, Chevy Chase, MD 20815-4520, Phone: (301)-656-3920, Fax: (301)-656-3815, email@asam.org, http://www.asam.org;
- Substance Abuse and Mental Health Services Administration (SAMHSA) is our government's resource agency for those suffering from such afflictions as alcoholism. Congress established SAMHSA in 1992 to make substance use and mental disorder information, services, and research more accessible. The agency has access to the latest research studies, and, in essence defines itself as, "works to improve the quality and availability of substance abuse prevention, alcohol and drug addiction treatment, and mental health services." They can be reached at http://www.samhsa.gov/ or by phoning (877)-SAMHSA-7 or (800)-487-4889 (TDD).

The Three Most Important Treatment Areas

For the woman seeking help, the three most important treatment areas are 1. detoxification

2. rehabilitation and finally if need be 3. long-term follow-up.

When a woman seeks help, she will find that there are more treatment facilities and detoxification centers for men than women. Treatment centers do not as a rule offer room for her children. It is usually the woman who has no family to call on for help, and, who consequently has no one with whom to leave her children, who needs the treatment center the most. This is especially true of the unwed mother. If her children run away because of an intolerable home situation, she is afraid to tell the family court that she is burdened with an arrestable disease called alcoholism for fear that the court will take away her children and place them in a state institution. She is not in the same position as a man, who, while seeking help, has a wife who watches the kids.

This situation appears to be improving for women. One sees judges more frequently giving suspended sentences to the woman alcoholic on the condition that she seek help. There is, too, a treatment center in Pennsylvania that accepts women with children.

We would like to describe in greater detail the actual resources available to the woman alcoholic and what she may experience in the various treatment areas.

Detoxification

Most treatment centers will only take a patient after a detoxification center or a hospital has detoxified her. A hospital gives in-patient care and is usually covered by hospital insurances such as Blue Cross. (National Health Care provides today hospitalization when needed. Furthermore, pre-existing conditions as alcoholism cannot keep anyone from receiving insurance.)

If the alcoholic has physical damage to any part of her body, is in danger of D.T.'s or convulsions, a hospital is a must. If an alcoholic does not need a hospital but has a "fear" of living without alcohol, an outpatient detoxification center may be desirable. Here the alcoholic will be able to talk to sympathetic people informed about alcoholism. Should she begin to shake or have any other physical discomfort, they know what doctors are on call. With proper medication, few people have to go through withdrawal symptoms.

Some detoxification centers will put their patients automatically on a tranquilizer to avoid acute nervousness. In conjunction with tranquilizers, the drug Antabuse ° (disulfiram) may be suggested. However, some therapists feel the patient should be sufficiently motivated to stop drinking without Antabuse because Antabuse may keep the alcoholic in the habit of taking drugs. Antabuse does not take away the urge to drink. It only promises, if you drink, a miserable aftermath. If Antabuse is seen as a friend, it will work for the alcoholic. If the patient seens Antabuse as an enemy, as another trick to keep her from drinking, then Antabuse will not work because it does not alter the consciousness process. The will to stop drinking has to come from within the patient.

Every attempt is made at the center to put the patient at ease and to give her helpful information. Here she may hear for the first time that alcoholism is a disease and not a disgrace. She may listen to other alcoholics, who have arrested their drinking, tell how they tried at first to give up drinking on their own and did not succeed. They might describe how, when on their own, the whole time they tried not to drink, their inner fantasies and thoughts were taken up with when they would have the first drink of the day. When blocked from the drink, they became nervous, anxious, irritable, and depressed.

She may have felt utterly alone in her situation. And now, it may be the first time, she hears that 9 million other people in this country have this disease and that many have resumed normal lives once they arrest their illness.

They will tell her about the latest relevant research that has been done on alcoholism and answer any question she or her family may have. The family, often more upset than the alcoholic, will receive reassurance, suggestions of resources for help in working out their problems, and advice on how to deal with the situation. Sometimes the family is advised that a breather for all may be good, and the alcoholic should be transferred to a half-way house or a treatment facility as the need may be.

The biggest problem in detoxification areas is getting the patient to stay in treatment, to go into rehabilitation, and to get more medical care if need be. If the patient is working or has a family she hesitates to leave, there are many out-patient clinics that will help her. If the patient leaves treatment too soon, she will be (or should be) made to feel welcome back anytime and should let the treatment center know under what conditions she would consider going back.

Rehabilitation

Some people will find that they need longer treatment and the support provided by a live-in treatment center. A treatment center should have no more than 25 people in it. Many treatment centers are co-ed, some just for women. More than just a substitute home, a treatment center provides new roots for the woman whose family and friends have deserted her. Even if she has a family, a treatment center is usually *better* than an unfriendly family. In such a center, a woman is treated with a respect she might not get at home. She can also get to know herself and learn to feel better about herself as an individual and as a woman.

Each treatment center has its own personality. A typical schedule follows:

7:00 A.M.	Get up.
7:30	Breakfast.
8:00	Clean up.
9:00	Group therapy.
10:00	Calisthenics—some centers encourage sports as tennis or swimming at the Y.
11:00	Personal counseling. (May include: family counseling, resolving legal problems, career counseling, talking with a social worker about what caused the alcoholic to drink. Discussing how free time can be converted from drinking time to coping or career time.)
12:00 P.M.	Lunch.
1:00	Rest period.

2:00	Lecture or movie on alcoholism.
3:00	Free activity which varies from day to day. (May include: vocational training, preparation for high school equivalency test or dusting off an up-to-now unused college degree; a course in personal finances; a discussion group on the feminine roles as seen by society, family, our employer, and ourselves.
4:00	Private appointments with dentist, general checkup, going to a job interview, shopping, sewing, or baking a cake for an AA meeting.
5:00	Dinner.
8:00	Community AA meeting with coffee and cake afterwards. (An outpatient clinic would include similar activities such as group therapy, calisthenics; personal counseling, AA meetings, and alcoholism education.)

For those who need it, medicines are administered by the treatment centers as prescribed by a physician. In these centers, the alcoholic continues to learn that alcoholism is a chronic disease which allows a recovery, an arrest of the symptoms, but rarely a cure. The patient comes to terms with her drinking. In other words, what caused her to drink? Were there other members in her family who drank and whom she is copying? Did she ever know how to have fun and to relax without alcohol? She learns what moral support she has within her and perhaps within her family. She tests out what works best to help her stay sober.

Her therapist emphasizes that she has and always has had the choices in life. The choice not to drink is up to her. Once the patient admits that she has a choice, a personal responsibility for that choice, and that her therapist would support, reinforce, encourage or, if need be, confront her with her choice, the patient feels stronger and more capable. The patient no longer feels she has to give up drinking by herself. Once she trusts the therapist, she will gain confidence that the therapist not only knows how to help her but wants to help her. She once again can find a much-needed sense of belonging. Often, the patient may even begin to talk about a renewed faith in the human spirit and her own capabilities.

She increases contact with her family and community. She may go home for a weekend. Or, the family may come and visit her and join one of the family group therapy sessions where everyone talks or listens as much as he or she may wish. If her marriage is bad and/or the children have real problems, she may be introduced to a family service or a mental health service near her home where she can continue to work out her problems. It is good for her to know that there are people near her home able and wanting to assist as long as she seeks them out.

On the average, the care at a treatment center may last from one to six months. Once discharged, the treatment center will welcome her to an alumni or transition group. She may be invited back two days a month to encourage other new members.

Long-Term Follow-Up

Should a patient have no home to go to after completing treatment and not be ready to live by herself, she would be invited to go to a halfway house. A halfway house is a home where she can live until she makes some permanent decisions. She might take a job while living in the halfway house. When she comes home in the evening, she is with people who understand what her past life has been like and who will give her the understanding she needs. If she feels too much pressure to slip back into past drinking habits, the people in the halfway house will know the resources in the neighborhood. The woman seeking long-term help will find herself confronted by a bewildering variety of possibilities. There are halfway houses, three-quarter way houses, one-quarter way houses, primary treatment centers, and on and on. Many of these represent little more than a quibble in semantics and, in any case, will vary from community to community and state to state.

Counselors in the Treatment Facilities

In all these treatment areas, the counselor plays a crucial part.

When a woman alcoholic receives counseling, it is very important that the counselor, especially a male counselor, recognize that a woman has an identity of her own that should be accepted. He must not forget that a woman's life is "arranged" very differently then that of a man's. Dr. A. N. Browne-Mayers and his co-workers explain it well in a report on a "Psychosocial Study of Hospitalized Middle Class Alcoholic Women." The study was done at the Department of Psychiatry Cornell Medical Center, Westchester Division, White Plains, New York.

The report says:

"After the woman alcoholic and her therapist have engaged in psychotherapy, we find that there is a residue. This residue, from our clinical observations, seems to be the frictions from the nurturing process that women are subject to in the United States. On the one hand, they are currently brought up to be sexy or not sexy. They are brought up so that they can perform as intelligent women, but they cannot appeal to men if they are bright. Therefore, they should be stupid. They are brought up to be able to work for a living, but, on the other hand, they are taught to become wise and become dependent on their husbands' financial success. They are taught to compete with men in the classroom; on the other hand, they are warned against competing with men. They are taught that they should be pretty and beautiful; on the other hand, they are taught not to be vain. The usual suburban housewife finds herself doing a vast number of tasks that frequently have little relationship to each other; for example, making sure that the children get to piano or art lessons and driving to the railroad station to pick up her husband at night or to get him there in the morning. In addition to these tasks, she must clean the house, cook the meals, do the washing, and finally, be the bright intellectual, stimulating woman who can be socially adept in the evening and a great sex partner at night. All these activities must necessarily lead to a certain confusion. This confusion would appear to be the residue we find after we have understood and treated the alcoholic woman."

Often women are treated by men who assume alcoholism is in all ways the same for her as for a man. For example, the counselor assumes that alcoholics drink in part to gain a sense of being big and strong and full of power. But we have seen that only men drink to gain a sense of masterfulness. Because society has taught us that aggressiveness is not becoming in a woman, women drink to feel less aggressive and more feminine. As women learn in our new society that they too can be a complete person, they won't feel obliged to hide their aggressive and competitive feelings.

A man who is trying to support his family may drink to counteract economic pressures. A woman who has no career other than being wife and mother may drink because she has trouble dealing with family life and the erotic aspects of living.

As has been pointed out, women may drink to deal with premenstrual cramps, postpartum depression, or to cope with a loss, such as a miscarriage or an operation on her ovaries. These need to be discussed with someone who understands and offers greater advice than a "Come on, snap out of it" attitude.

The alcoholic woman may be an unmarried woman with several children. She may feel, no matter how much empathy a male therapist shows her, that he sees her as a loose woman. She feels, what does he know about getting pregnant? About being so lonely that it renders you helpless? Unless he has deep insight, *as unprofessional as these feelings may be*, he may experience a certain amount of disgust at a woman who would let herself get into such a predicament. There are all kinds of people in the helping profession, and many allow an extension of their own feelings.

In addition, male staffers may view a woman as someone who is physically limited and does everything to please and attract men. Even if she does not have a family to go back to, he may encourage a "new but stable relationship with a man." Indirectly, he contributes to her not feeling whole without a man, leaving her open to a "grab the first one" attitude. The same male staffer may treat the male patient as someone who may need to get back to his job and then to his family position. If the female patient has to take a job, the male staffer may see her in the traditional role of secretary, file clerk, or nurse's aide, etc.

The helping professions consider an alcoholic woman more difficult to treat than an alcoholic man. Her pent-up resentments make her a difficult patient. Being a woman, she does not have to put up in public that brave front that is expected of a man. A man can stay home, complain to the family, and let himself be nursed by his wife. A woman has to go out of the house to be nursed. Whether she is in a hospital, a rehabilitation facility, or in a halfway house she satisfies her dependent needs and hostile feelings by sulking or complaining. Without fail, she sees her own pain as being worse than that of others with the same pain. She claims often that she gets the least attention of any patient.

Women who are recovered alcoholics have told this author that it is always more upsetting to see a woman come apart than a man because there is so much more to come apart. She uses makeup, colors her hair, adorns herself with jewelry and fashionable clothes. When a man drinks, he doesn't have to worry about running mascara, and he usually has a woman in his life who will clean his clothes so he won't lose his job. If a woman is dirty, she is left dirty. Counselors, nurses, and social workers who like to think of the woman of today as someone special, more self-reliant than her mother was, may well be as disgusted by her as the physicians. If she is not a modern woman, she is at least expected to make her home comfortable and secure.

As the counselor (as well as nurses, doctors, and others in the helping profession) works with the alcoholic, the latent wish to be dependent (and perhaps to drink) may be aroused in some. Rather than admit their fears, it is easier to express their fear by showing disgust for the alcoholic patient. Alcoholic women who recognize the counselor's or the staff's attitude have more self-hate and act out more than those who receive compassion. Is it any wonder then that no matter how ready a treating facility is to welcome her, she becomes wary of that welcome? Our modern facilities may have to work twice as hard to make her feel truly welcomed. It can be done.

Because the alcoholic in treatment seeks out models for her recovery process, the ideal treatment center has both males and females on staff. Each play an important role. All the more reason that the right male staffers are invaluable. If the male staffer treats her with respect, it is a worthwhile experience for her. A woman may feel uncomfortable with a male counselor because she may have had bad experiences with men. A perceptive male counselor will soon recognize this feeling and get her to ventilate it.

The woman counselor plays an invaluable role, too. If a female counselor who will serve as her model is consistent in her moods, her chores, her grooming, then she is living proof that a female alcoholic can recover. The therapeutic model need not have an academic degree, but may have had the experience of having lived in a recovery center herself. If the counselor sticks by her patient through her crises, her anxiety attacks, her self-hate, her rediscovery of her true self, her ups and downs and feeds her, spoonful by spoonful, the realities of her life, the counselor model will succeed in healing the wounds that kept her patient drinking.

Some treatment centers have, during their staff meetings, consciousness-raising meetings to test their own feelings. They ask themselves: Are they too bossy with their patients? Are they seeking attainable goals for their patients?

Many counselors are their patients' pathfinders to new lives. The unhappiest and the most seemingly hopeless cases find that they can and deserve to make it in life. One can only understand and *feel* this after meeting some of the recovered women.

Case History: Betty

Betty, age 29, is a typical example of a woman who came to a treatment center full of hope. If she could once and for all stop drinking, maybe, she thought, she could regain custody of her children who the court had awarded to the father when the divorce came through. Her hope was unrealistic. A very dependent, talented, sensitive person, she had married a grammar school teacher the year she graduated from high school. He was tall, handsome, and seemed to know how to handle every situation. But the man who Betty saw as a pillar of strength was really a cold, aloof person.

After their third child was born, the family moved to a new town where her husband had been offered a better job. Betty knew no one in the new town. She was frequently alone because her husband in addition to his grammar school job took a job teaching at night in a local community college. Betty felt tied down with the children while her husband was teaching women younger than she. When he was home, he ate mostly in his study because the children bothered him, and he could work on his papers while he ate. Betty began to drink. Her husband lectured her on her responsibilities and "character."

Betty felt guilty that she drank, and often answered, "Yes, I know I am no good." Betty forgot to feed the children, to even bathe herself. Her husband met Judy, a student in the community college. Judy helped to take care of the children while she shook her head at Betty's drinking. Betty lost her husband to helpful Judy. In the divorce proceedings, the judge awarded the children to the father and his new bride.

Betty is now in a treatment center. She has no hope of getting her children back because they have grown to love Judy. When Betty gets back on her feet, she will have no friends, no responsive husband, no children. The pain of losing her children is great. No one is going to praise Betty for being normal again. Can such a woman as Betty pick up the pieces?

The answer is yes.

When Betty came into the treatment center, she had a morbid kind of self-pity. Her pain and her anger was just too great for her to concentrate on anything. She felt shamed by her husband and hurt by her children. She kept saying, "It's my fault that I lost the children. Drinking ruined my whole life."

Betty, like most alcoholics, thought that she had only one problem—drink. But when she gave up drinking, she found that she was still the same person with the same problems. She had to face the fact that her marriage was not good—whether she drank or did not drink. She had to recognize that the image she had of herself and the reality of her situation were markedly different.

Betty started to drink only when she got married. Her husband was very critical of her so she began to drink socially to boost her ego. Her husband, by acting aloof and cold, confirmed her feelings of inferiority. Her depression should have told her that something was wrong in her family. But depression can take as long as five years to be recognized and it can block out the truth and cause a woman as well as a man to counteract the depression by drinking. Even if Betty arrests her drinking, she will have to deal with her depression. Since alcohol is a depressant, it makes any depression (for that matter, any problem) that much worse. If, when arresting her drinking, she overlooks her depression, she may have a drinking relapse.

Her dependency on her husband came from an alternation of love and rejection that she experienced in her youth. Her father had walked out on her mother and her when she was eight years old. She had loved her father, a jovial man who drank heavily. The hurt was great, but Betty identified with him rather than with her mother who cried a lot. Her mother, rather than tell her what was wrong, just complained in general without defining what had happened in the family.

As Betty continued to think about her marriage, she came to realize that she had been in an emotional anesthesia. She had shown no feelings toward those involved with her. Her husband didn't mind and didn't do anything about her drinking as long as she functioned. While she was at the beginning stages of her alcoholism, she was an excellent housekeeper. She felt used and abused. How marvelous it was for Betty to know that others in the treatment center needed to hear her story. It made her feel for the first time since she had married that she too had something worthwhile to say.

It took Betty a long time to tell "her story" to the group in the treatment center. Her story came out in spurts, and the counselor and the group slowly made her realize that her story was not so awful. While she was married, she felt rejected. She didn't protest this feeling because she felt low about herself, and she thought no one would want to bother to help her. Betty kept saying, "I know my neighbors thought I was an awful wife and mother.

Her counselor explained to Betty that only as she begins to see herself as worth helping can she begin to reach out to her therapist and to her AA sponsor. She has to desire health and self-esteem for herself. *She has to keep telling herself that for herself she is the most important person in the world.* Coping with alcoholism to please her children, her husband and the judge who placed her children away from her will not work.

The women in the treatment center made Betty feel that in this therapy group, she is a very important person. Here are some of the

THE DRINKING WOMAN: REVISITED

comments that were made in the therapy group by Betty, the counselor, and her group and taped for this book. It is fascinating to see how closely these comments support the observations the counselor made with Betty in private.

Betty: "I tried sleeping last night without taking my tranquilizers, and I didn't close my eyes. I felt so alone. Always alone."

Fellow Patient: "Think of the power of love, of God. Take an inventory of yourself. You have yourself and you are a very important person."

Betty: "Myself? I can't even live with myself without tranquilizers."

Fellow Patient: "You have options in life. You don't have to feel helpless and angry and take tranquilizers. You can do something about your situation."

Betty: "Every morning I wake up tired. Drained. Every chore here exhausts me. And all the time I am angry, angry, angry."

Fellow Patient: "If you can't deal with that anger and let it rot within you, you may decide to drink again."

Betty: "It's my children. (She cries hard, very hard.) The worst of it is nobody, nobody needs me."

Fellow Patient: "You can fill your life with a career, make new friends through AA and our treatment center. You can reach out to other women who are in the same situation."

Fellow Patient: "The same thing happened to me as to you, Betty. No judge let me get cured. He gave the children to my husband and my mother-in-law. I have been here three months now. I had to get in touch with the pain of the loss and mourn and mourn—just the way I would for the death of a loved one."

Fellow Patient: "Listen, this loss of yours can be a blessing because it is a turning point in your life. For the first time in your life, you have an opportunity to find out what you want because obviously no one cared before or your marriage would have worked out."

Fellow Patient: "You might just be luckier than Judy because Judy now has your cold husband. What has Judy got? She is nothing but a housekeeper for a man who needs to be seen as father. He'll always marry sick and weak women who'll worship him and whom he can continually teach."

Fellow Patient: "Yeah. Both you and Judy have one thing in common, a father fixation. You still need a father."

Fellow Patient: "Judy may not drink alcohol like you, but in desperation, she'll turn to something."

Fellow Patient: "What was the matter with you anyway? You were so dependent on everything outside you and not on the strength within you. I mean you could have dealt with your situation. You could have taken courses yourself. You could have taken a part-time job. If you felt blue, you could have done volunteer work where you would be with other people."

Counselor: "Betty has to decide what Betty wants. Maybe she doesn't love her children. She has to look at the *whole* Betty. In this case, she is blaming herself too much. It's the same old story—'women abandon'—'men walk out.' Why didn't a child protest that her mother was leaving?"

Fellow Patient: "Besides, many people don't raise their own children and are called mothers. Look at the people who send their children to boarding school and claim it is good for the children."

Fellow Patient: "You can give warmth to children without having them. Good examples are "single" teachers."

Fellow Patient: "When your children are older, they'll understand you better, and if you have worked out a life of your own, they will take pride in you."

Fellow Patient: "Besides, you are young. and might marry again and raise another family."

Counselor: "You are projecting that Betty will want another husband and children; if she gets her own identity, she might choose not to be anyone's wife, not to have any more children. She may want a career and a life of her own; fulfillment is not always husband and children. A man cannot fulfill you. Your children can't fulfill you. They are only a part of your whole life and only then if you choose it."

A New Attitude

In the treatment center, there were a number of female therapists, some who themselves were single, some who were arrested alcoholics, others who were successfully married career women. They gave Betty a variety of models of female strength she had never seen. She saw that women can be on their own. They can support themselves.

Betty must learn to feel better as a woman, as a she person. At present, she doesn't feel whole without a man. If she waits a while to pick a man, she can work on herself. If she enters a relationship with a man at this stage of her treatment, all her energies will go into making the relationship work instead of solving her problems. She will end up losing. The treatment center offers Betty the time she needs. Before she leaves the treatment center, she will have had experience in the working world. When she becomes financially independent, she will not be in a position of having to get married for support. No one can hurt her. She can truly feel good about being a woman free of drink. When she has nothing to do on Sunday, she will be coming to the treatment center—or dinner, perhaps bringing a cake she baked as a hostess gift. She will continue to go to the weekly AA meeting at the treatment center as well as to the one in her community. If something bothers her on her job or if she feels depressed, she may visit a counselor at the treatment center to whom she feels close and discuss it with her. The treatment center may invite her on a Sunday to discuss with the women her job, her new life, and answer questions.

Betty will continue to learn about herself even after she leaves the treatment center. Personal growth is not a one-time thing but a continual process.

Updates

- Concerned about suicide? Think twice and phone 1-(800)-273-TALK (8255) TTY: 1-(800)-799-4889. They have the utmost compassion, are on your side, and will help you.
- Alcoholics needing treatment will often avoid going for help by saying "That's not me. I only drink once a week. I may get drunk but it's just once a week." Or, "I went to one Alcoholics Anonymous meeting and the people there were different than me. Most were very educated and had jobs. I am just a high school dropout who works as a waitress." Or "I went to an AA meeting. I am an educated person with a job and these people are all working in fields I would not con-

sider." Several facts can be gathered from these comments. These are all excuses to avoid realizing that one needs to take action. Another detail is that one can always choose to go to another AA group if the first one did not suit the individual. Just think if you had cancer and were sent to join a group to discuss your feelings about cancer would you really care about these people's background rather than the all-important reality that you are all trying to deal with cancer and hoping to reach remission.

- If you are having a hard time admitting to yourself that you need to give up drinking the very circumstance that you are reading this material means that your are thinking about it. According to Prochaska et al (1992) one model suggests five stages an alcoholic and/or multi-substance abuser goes through. The first is a precontemplation which consists of "do I really have a problem and if, is it really serious?" The next stage is contemplative where the patient thinks, "Yes, there does seem to be problem but am I going to do something about it? I am not ready to make a commitment to change even though I know there is a problem." The third stage is called preparation. The alcoholic cuts down on the drinking and looks for help from a substance abuse facility. The final two stages, action and maintenance are the goals the patient needs to reach. Here the patient goes into treatment, gives up drinking and educates herself on how to avoid relapses.

- An alternative to Alcoholics Anonymous may be Women For Sobriety. Quite a few women have found it helpful to attend both AA and WFS. WFS describes itself as, "—unique in that it is an organization of women for women. We are not affiliated with any other recovery organization and stand on our own principles and philosophies. We recognize each woman's necessity for self-discovery. WFS offers a variety of recovery tools to guide a woman in developing coping skills which focus on emotional growth, spiritual growth, self-esteem, and a healthy lifestyle. Our vision is to encourage all women in developing personal growth and continued abstinence through the [13 step] 'New Life' Program." Their contact is Women For Sobriety, Inc.Office: (215)-536-8026 Fax: (215)-538-9026; P.O. Box 618, Quakertown, PA 18951; www.womenforsobriety.org/. WFS has annual conferences where women trying to cope with their problems gather and receive useful information.

- Need an alcohol free residence? Visit The National Alliance for Recovery Residences
- http://narronline.org/resources, telephone: (855)-355-NARR (6277) or get in touch with The Sober Living Network P.O. Box 5235, Santa Monica, Ca. 90409 (310)-396-5270. These are nonprofit residences founded to help those suffering from addiction to get back on their feet.
- The saying that alcoholics have to hit rock bottom before they can be helped is a myth. Often at that point an alcoholic is so sick that it is difficult to get her physical being back to normal. Dr. Thomas Beresford, a physician in the field of addiction and who wrote the introduction to this book, emphasizes that when we drink alcohol reaches every part of the body and therefore influences our complete wellbeing. It is a well known statistic that alcoholics do not live as long as abstainers or social drinkers. Friedman and Martin repeat these findings in many categories in their book, *The Longevity Project*.
- INTERVENTION is when family and friends with the help of a professional counselor talk eye to eye with the member in crisis because of her drinking problem. Intervention helps to stop denial which is "the most destructive aspects of addiction. It denies healing and it involves lying" (*For Teenagers Living With A Parent Who Abuses Alcohol/Drugs*, chapter 10). Once the family and the friends of the alcoholic make the decision to confront the alcoholic they are no longer the enablers. It is imperative that the intervention be done with a trained interventionist. The interventionist counselor will gather with the family and friends for several sessions before

the actual intervention to get the alcoholic's history, explain how the alcoholic will be addressed and decide with her family and friends where the alcoholic will go immediately after the intervention: to a hospital, rehabilitation center, a daily outpatient clinic or join Alcoholics Anonymous. The group will also discuss with the interventionist counselor what will be done if the alcoholic does not cooperate. Will the group tell her, "We won't pay your bills anymore and you will become homeless." Or "Your children will have to be placed with other relatives or in foster care." Or "We will no longer when you have a hangover lie to your employer why you are not coming to work." Telephone Family First Intervention (888) 743-9920 or (888) 275-5072, and online visit www.intervention.com or phone (800) 789-1605.

- Women alcoholics sometimes live with a "functioning" alcoholic husband. "Functioning" alcoholics are those who drink heavily but who can still maintain their jobs and other outside activities without revealing their strong need for alcohol. The wife may, while drinking with him, reach the advanced stages of alcoholism more quickly than her drinking husband. Being a heavy drinker he may not notice that she passes out when drinking heavily, and not realize that she lost her job because of her drinking.
- There are various reasons that the family needs to go into treatment as one unit. It not only helps the alcoholic to see why she needs to stop drinking but it also helps each member of the family to understand how living with an alcoholic has influenced each of those in her life. Are the children using pot because they feel "it is better than alcohol?" Is the father taking anti-depressants to shut out his problems? It is significant as well for the family as whole to see whether their life style contributes to their daughter's/mother's/wife's/girlfriend's drinking. One therapist explained how he had a hard time making the family of his patient, Mona, who he was treating for alcohol addiction, understand that their dinner parties that involved wine drinking was difficult for

Mona. She had to continually explain to their guests why she was not drinking. Furthermore the smell of wine made her want to drink. He suggested that they rethink their Saturday night activities.

- Psychiatrists specializing in addiction often work with parole boards, probation officers, and pretrial services to plan appropriate mandated treatment for women diagnosed as alcoholics who are a danger to themselves as well as to the community, but who are now willing to cooperate.
- Alcoholism is a chronic disease and the patient may need to stay for the rest of her life in a group such as Alcoholics Anonymous to maintain sobriety.
- Physicians specializing in alcoholism will often use the Addiction Severity Index (McLellan et al. 1992). ASI assesses a patient's amount of drinking, the legal status (underage, adult, prison record, driving under the influence citations), medical status (is she healthy or are there indications of cirrhosis of the liver, diabetes, heart palpitations etc.), employment/support status, family/social relationships, and psychiatric status (depression, anger etc.) All this information will help the physician to determine the treatment needed. If a woman is drinking because she is depressed or overwhelmed by poverty, a bad marriage, demanding parents the doctor can help her work out a plan to make her life controllable and place her in the appropriate treatment for her addiction. Not all conditions of alcoholism require hospitalization. Today there is a varied source of outpatient clinics helping alcoholics regain their health and sobriety. The patient herself often feels relieved to be able to talk to a compassionate professional clinician. Doris, a mother, career woman, and wife, who finally acknowledged when she was in her 50s that she does have a drinking problem explained, "What helped me the most was having a plan as to how I was going to give up drinking. I decided that I would attend Alcoholics Anonymous, see privately a therapist to discuss some personal problems and go for a week to a yoga retreat. It was tough, really tough but I

promised myself if I follow the plan it would get better. After the yoga retreat where I talked to other women trying to get their lives to be better I began to see the possibility of never drinking again." Karen's story is completely different. "I began to see my life change also once I made a plan. I was homeless when I decided to do something about my drinking. I lived on the street in a box over an air grill. I would beg for money with which I bought cheap liquor. One day a woman stopped and said there was an Alcoholics Anonymous meeting in an hour in the church at the end of the street and there would be lots of coffee and pastry. I came for the food. I also listened to the stories. I kept going to the meetings for the pastry and coffee. It took many meetings but eventually apart from telling my story at AA I also decided to go to a free class that taught how to get out of poverty. I was able to move in to a woman's residence which gave me a job cleaning while I continued to go to Alcoholics Anonymous and attend a computer class which eventually got me a job I like. It wasn't just going to AA but also making a plan how I could better my life that got me back on my feet."

- When seeking care either from a physician, a psychologist, or a psychiatrist an alcoholic patient should ask the following questions: "Have you yourself ever attended an Alcoholics Anonymous meeting?" *The American Psychiatric Publishing Textbook of Substance Abuse Treatment 4th edition* pages 82–88, 382 very sensibly points out that because alcoholism is a chronic disease the patient will have to maintain her sobriety once her treatment is completed with such a group as AA. It is therefore vital that her counselor or therapist be familiar with AA and work in union with the 12 steps. If the alcoholic is seeking help from a psychiatrist or internist because medication may have to be prescribed it is wise to check that all and any of these professionals are members of The American Society of Addiction Medicine. ASAM's members specialize in addiction and are aware of the most recent studies.

- There are basically three stages of addiction treatment which A. Thomas McLellan, Ph.D. identifies in the chapter, Evolution in Addiction Treatment Concepts and Methods in the book, *The American Psychiatric Publishing Textbook of Substance Abuse Treatment 4th edition.*

Step one: Detoxification/Stabilization

For those experiencing serious withdrawal symptoms as well as physiological and/or emotional shakiness appropriate medication accompanied with rest and motivational therapy is recommended in a hospital or residential setting. The motivational therapy will hopefully prepare the patient for continued rehabilitation.

Step two: Rehabilitation

Treatments vary. The author of this book, *The Drinking Woman*, would like to say that after visiting many Alcoholics Anonymous groups as a guest she has noted alcoholics who do not need Step One may go to Alcoholics Anonymous on their own and succeed without outside care. However, others with special needs go to psychiatrists to receive individual counseling and analysis of their emotional problems. A psychiatrist may as well prescribe medicine for depression and cravings. There are also residential rehabilitation programs such as Betty Ford Clinic, Phoenix House and others listed with The National Alliance for Recovery Residences and The Sober Living Network. Rehabilitation treatment may consist of various treatments given cooperatively with individual therapy, medical prescriptions, and group therapy.

Step three: Maintaining sobriety

The doctor or counselor will determine if medication needs to be continued. The patient will carry on her group therapy and be aware of danger signals warning her of an impending relapse.
- There are medication such as disulfiram, naltrexone and acamprosate that may block the desire to drink. These medications need to be taken under the supervision of a physician specializing in addiction.

- According to Dr. A. T. McLellan in *The American Psychiatric Publishing Textbook of Substance Abuse Treatment 4th edition*, page 103 most people seeking counseling for addiction such as heavy drinking end up in group therapy which might include orientation groups in which patients introduce themselves and learn about group therapy. There are also therapy groups to work out addiction problems and groups catering to relapse avoidance. Dr. McLellan points out, "—most studies of patients in treatment reveal that very few patients actually receive medical or social services beyond general counseling." A central factor determining a patient's need to be hospitalized is the gravity of her alcohol withdrawal syndrome (Delirium Tremens, loss of consciousness and general physical condition). Such drugs as diazepam or other benzodiazepines are administered by a physician to ease withdrawal syndromes. Statistics tell us that many alcoholics can stop drinking without being hospitalized. The craving may be strong but may not necessarily include hallucinations, disorientation or shaking.
- If you suffer from alcoholism you may have more than one problem and may require what is called wrap around services which may consist of parenting services, psychiatric care, safe housing. A social worker or a counselor may help you discover these services. Fellow Alcoholics Anonymous members sometimes know where to find such support. Another good source of information is your local mental health department.
- SAMHSA is our government's resource agency for those suffering from such afflictions as alcoholism. Congress established the Substance Abuse and Mental Health Services Administration (SAMHSA) in 1992 to make substance use and mental disorder information, services, and research more accessible. The agency has access to the latest research studies, and, in essence defines itself as, "works to improve the quality and availability of substance abuse prevention, alcohol and drug addiction treatment, and mental health

services." They can be reached at http://www.samhsa.gov/ or by phoning (877)-SAMHSA-7 or (800)-487-4889 (TDD). Another agency mentioned many times in this book and which you may want to reach directly for further information is the National Institute on Alcohol Abuse and Alcoholism (NIAAA). Sponsored by our government's National Institutes of Health U.S. "to integrate resources and expertise to advance substance use, abuse, and addiction research and public health outcomes." They can be reached at NIAAA/NIH, 5635 Fishers Lane, Room 2013, Rockville, MD, 20852, telephone (301)-443-2594 or CRAN@mail.nih.gov.

CHAPTER 14

GETTING READY TO FACE THE WORLD AGAIN

Many alcoholic women like Betty find themselves "single" once they have succeeded in arresting their drinking. Their husbands may have walked out on them while they were actively drinking. Other women were not married when they started to drink. Once in therapy, many single women confided they were too shy to meet men, afraid of their female identity, or felt their personality had scared men off. Others may be widows who started to drink when their husbands died. And now that these widows have arrested their drinking, they have to come to terms with their loneliness. Those who are still married may have to face a marriage that was never good to begin with. Such a woman may need to go into marriage counseling together with her husband to see how they can strengthen their relationship.

But what about the single woman who thinks all through her stay in the treatment center: "When I leave here I will be alone again"? What about the woman whose husband not only is gone, but who never had children, or whose children are grown and gone? She may think, "I remember how hard it was managing and making friends before I drank. It was so tough it made me drink."

As a woman discusses her status, she finds that once she is a recovered alcoholic, she may still be bothered by the same social problems she had before she started to drink. If she drank, because she was shy, she will still be shy. If she stayed single to support mother and keep her company, her life will not change once she stops drinking. If she drank because she was too embarrassed to face the fact that she is a lesbian, when she stops drinking her affections toward women will be the same.

The progressive treatment centers are helping their single members to clarify in their minds what is best for their needs. Singles are asked to respond and reach out more in their relationships to people in general rather than to date right away. If a woman had a poor opinion of herself, she may keep herself from meeting a satisfactory partner. Just to have a man, she may choose an affair without any real emotion. All these women who are seeking a more meaningful life are asked to look into the quality rather than the quantity of their dating.

Many women are asked in these groups whether they are aware of the factors which, before arresting their drinking, made them reluctant to date without alcohol. Did alcohol make them feel more popular? Prettier? More experienced? Liberated?

Once this pressure, "I must have a man," is alleviated, a woman can begin to see herself as an individual.

It is important for all single women to have some insight into what makes them tick. It can help them to further their careers and to have better relations with their extended families (in-laws, cousins, etc.). It can also help them to cope better with their feelings in moments of stress and to be more relaxed on dates.

Without realizing it, some women antagonize their dates. Men, of course, are not free of this game either. But once we know ourselves as women, we will gain an insight which will give us the opportunity to form positive relationships in all situations.

Envious Ellen

Ellen met her boy friend in the department store where they both worked. He was the buyer for sporting goods while Ellen was the buyer for women's gloves. Since the store was in New York City, Ellen was able to visit all the glove importers and manufacturers right in the city. Sporting goods are not manufactured in the city, and her boy friend had to go on business trips. Ellen felt envious. She did not recognize her envy. She blamed the store for allowing more travel expenses to the sporting goods department. She accused her boy friend of conniving to get these trips out of town. Ellen especially expressed these thoughts to her boy friend after several cocktails. She made biting comments about how he enjoyed himself on his trips out of town. Her boy friend could not take Ellen's behavior and dropped her. Ellen never wondered why he dropped her. As far as Ellen was concerned, everyone was luckier than she. They had nicer apartments or nicer clothes than she. Ellen did not keep her friends for long.

Ellen's envy was developed when she was a small child. Ellen used to watch her younger brother suck at their mother's breast. Her mother used to comment how much better he sucked than Ellen who, as an infant, had always spat up and many times rejected her feedings. As Ellen grew older, she learned that her brother was permitted to do more than she. He was sent to private school to get a better education while she was sent to public school. Thus, the pattern "envy" was nurtured from childhood on. Ellen's experience with her boy friend—"He can travel for the store; I can't"—was an expression of this envy. For Ellen, it was a repeat of "My brother can go to private school, and I can't go to private school." Ellen was still seeking her mother's love. She was in essence saying, "I want you, Mother, to love me as much as you love my brother."

If travel meant so much to her, she could have changed jobs. But no matter what job Ellen would take, the envy would still be there.

Jealous Susan

Susan met her boy friend at a community dance. He worked in a law firm that handled many divorce cases. Without any proof, Susan was convinced that he had affairs with the divorced women involved in the cases he handled, even though most of them were much older than he. Susan would question him in a prying, angry, hostile manner. When out for dinner, after a drink or two she would ask in great detail about what he did during his lunch hour. Her questions were sometimes insulting. He got fed up and left.

Susan had grown up as an only child. Her mother was very possessive of Susan's father. She would put Susan down by such comments as "Look at the little girl trying to play the grown up in front of Daddy." Her mother also excluded Susan from many family affairs such as excursions, vacations, etc. when she could have included her. Susan thought her extreme jealous nature was something she had been born with.

Of course, we all have the emotions of jealousy and envy. It is just when it is so out of proportion that it colors our personality that we should follow it to its source. We have to see the problem and be willing to do something about it. These two brief case histories help us see why Susan and Ellen acted as they did. It is never just one event in our lives that determines our personality pattern. Our emotions are colored by the ways in which society, our neighborhood, and the people in school have all affected us. Childhood experiences can result in making us aloof, afraid to show emotion. All of us learn early in life to protect ourselves from hurt. If we get rejected too often by the boys, we are going to say, "Who cares anyway?" Extreme experiences can turn us into a cold fish. A good example are victims of continual unemployment. Rather than face the fear of being turned down for a job, they would rather sit home and watch TV. A girl who has had too many hurts in society would rather stay home. Or when she does meet someone, she will insulate herself by not showing too much feeling. "What a bore!" her companions will say as they seek someone livelier.

We have all met the other extreme, too, someone who talks too much. Who hasn't heard someone complain at one time or another, "She talks like a waterfall." These women usually talk themselves out of company. It may be a passing phase, as they attempt to compensate for symptoms of unhappiness. Such people may talk a lot about their childhood because they want to return to the carefree period of their lives when someone took good care of them. Other times they may be trying to compensate for their unhappiness by painting a terrific life in their minds. "We used to have such fun at our summer house." While it may bore the rest of the crowd she is out with, she is portraying for herself the happy life she never had.

Temper Tantrum Ruth

The list of ways in which we may antagonize people is long. Among alcoholics, temper is a frequent problem. Temper can be traced to accumulated tensions. We may not enjoy our jobs. If we have arrested our drinking recently, we may still miss alcohol. We may feel our families have treated us unjustly.

Ruth had just arrested her drinking. She was in AA, and she was seeing a social worker who was trying to help her straighten out her life. Ruth's husband had walked out on her. Her teenaged son who lived with her was not doing well in school, her own parents were not giving her the encouragement she needed, and Ruth still missed alcohol. She went to AA meetings every night and to her social worker once a week. She realized that while her parents and her husband had not always been fair to her, there were many ways in which she herself could have handled her life better. Ruth had many emotions, and she was working her problems out.

In the meantime, all these frustrations made her explode at the least provocation. Because she had a good job which she wanted to keep, she forced herself to be pleasant at work. Therefore, when the women in the office decided to go to dinner one night, they asked Ruth to go along. The evening was a disaster. First, the women went to a Chinese restaurant. Ruth hated Chinese food, but she did not have the courage to say anything. After dinner, the women decided to go to a movie. When they decided on a movie Ruth didn't want to see, she exploded. If she had been pleasant about her reasons for not wanting to see the movie, the women might have agreed with her. But for Ruth, it was the straw that broke the camel's back. She had no strength left to be nice. What had got her angry had nothing to do with the source. Her anger was displaced. Ruth let all her accumulated tensions out on her newfound friends. They couldn't believe such childish behavior or understand it since they didn't know about Ruth's background.

Many treatment centers will tell of innumerable instances in which emotions have flared up among women over a seemingly unimportant incident such as one woman innocently borrowing a book or nail polish from another without asking. The flare ups in most cases have nothing to do with the borrowed book or nail polish. It is only an outlet for the pent-up tensions.

Angry Becky

Anger, too, is an emotion that can hinder our social intercourse. Sometimes if we are extremely angry, we transfer that anger to a scapegoat. "I can't stand blacks, Jews, etc."

Angry Becky was such a woman. She would always find something in her friends that made her angry and therefore unpleasant. Becky's tongue made her lose many a friend.

Becky was a hard worker in a dress factory. She showed tremendous organizational and managing ability. When the foreman of the assembly line retired Becky was given his job. Becky was thrilled. It meant a raise in her salary and hope for a successful career. However, whenever something went wrong Becky, although she knew how to rectify the situation, always did it in an angry manner. If a sewing machine would breakdown she would curse the one who had been using it. Or, if a worker didn't show up for work she would make such comments as, "Well we all know her kind are lazy."

Becky always had a few beers with her lunch and she became known for her "afternoon language." Becky eventually was transferred to the factory's stockroom where she did not have to deal with people.

Anger such as Becky's can develop early in childhood. When a parent is impatient and uses excessive punishments, that youngster will often displace her anger on others. Becky told her therapist, "Both my parents believed in spanking children. If my room wasn't clean my mother, rather than show me how to do it, would hit me. My father too had a fast hand. But if I showed anger mom said that it isn't ladylike. My brother, who also got hit, was commended if he showed his anger "like a man" by fighting the boys on the playground. I just got smacked by my mother if I went out and had a fight. As I got older I took pleasure in scolding, ridiculing, or tattling. Once I started to date I became real bitchy. I would say things like, "Service is terrible here." "I can cook better than this." "What ridiculous decor!" "How can you say such ridiculous things?" "Did you see that awful girl at the pool today?"

When such a woman as Becky drinks she may really feel relaxed enough to let go of her pent-up anger.

Personalities Can Change

Personalities can be improved. We do not have to go through life being antagonistic. We all have moments of envy, jealousy, or anger. Sometimes rightly so. Why shouldn't someone who feels her family didn't treat her right have a moment of envy when she sees someone who was showered with love. However, we do not have to make that the symbol of our life.

We can change.

It is one of the functions of the treatment centers, AA, family service, psychiatric treatment, and all the other helping agencies to make us aware that we are not the only ones who have these problems. We can talk them out until the problems no longer bother us. All of a sudden we are more interested in tomorrow than in yesterday. If we hear the woman sitting next to us tell us how her husband showed her no compassion when she was ill, our anger, our envy, our jealousy is changed for that moment to compassion for her. And that moment changes us, too.

The ones who are best equipped to point out this new outlook on life are not always the professionals who may be happily married, but fellow female alcoholics who do live alone successfully. One treatment center in Pennsylvania has a blind therapist who lives alone: In a not so subtle way, he gives the message to his patients that "medical complications are no excuse for feeling sorry for yourself."

Until we can begin to date, it is well worth the trouble to see ourselves first as we are. Perhaps we will discover we really don't want to date men. Or, yes, perhaps, we would like to resettle ourselves with a new husband. One counselor in Massachusetts explained, "We give priority to different lifestyles. Women are helped not to feel guilty when they masturbate. Not every woman is made to feel she should date. Or, if it is better for two women to live together, we give couple treatment to them." Another treatment center in Pennsylvania dismisses its women in pairs. They take apartments together and share their costs together; If they date, fine. If not, they are not lonely. They belong somewhere. Other treatment centers are even encouraging their women to learn how to change storm windows or fix leaks. One therapist said, "It's as simple as survival versus non-survival."

Meeting Mr. Right

For the woman who wants to meet men, dating can be a problem. If she has just arrested her drinking, she may find it hard in a dating situation to explain why she can't have a drink. Not so many years ago, if a woman didn't drink, it was accepted without a second thought. Today, a woman who doesn't drink is considered immature or unsociable. One divorced woman in a therapy group said, "Before I married the very first time (about 40 years ago), girls used to drink little because they were coy and protecting themselves. But as contraceptives came in, they let their hair down and drank 'like a man.'" This is especially true in small towns where the only entertainment may be the local bar, night spots, country clubs, or the Saturday night gathering in a private home. Seventeen magazine recently sent out a questionnaire to a few girls who act as stringers for the magazine throughout the United States. They were asked to distribute a questionnaire among their colleagues. Although no conclusive facts can be drawn from this questionnaire, Seventeen noticed that many girls who lived in small towns said they drank when they did "because there was nothing else to do." While those who lived in areas where there were activities available stated that drinking was a minor social activity.

In our present society if a woman does not drink, she feels she should give a "reason" for turning down a drink. R. Straus and S. D. Bacon, in their classical book, *Drinking in College*, very aptly point out that many women drink because they feel it is social, they will mix better, and that if they don't drink, they may just not be asked out again.

This attitude is hard for alcoholic women trying to mix with new friends. Women who are alcoholics have found that dating or gathering on an informal basis—picnics, church, clubs, sticking to AA groups, and making friends within AA—alleviates the pressure to drink. We all need a sense of belonging to a family or a group when we date. Just for an alcoholic woman to know that she does have a roommate, does belong to AA, can discuss her feelings in a sympathetic group, will make her more particular when she dates.

Recovered alcoholics have particular needs and must learn to be assertive or men may make them feel put down. He may encourage her to drink. Some men when they hear a woman is an alcoholic may automatically assume she is a "loose" woman like all those women in the bars. She'll drop those men quickly enough because with the help of AA and treatment centers, psychiatrists and other helping agencies, she knows she has a choice. A better choice.

EPILOGUE: REBUILDING

Remember Betty who cried because the judge had ruled that her children should live with her ex-husband and his new wife, Judy?

Betty stayed in the treatment center six months. While in the treatment center, she became friendly with another woman, and the two took an apartment together at the end of their treatment. Betty got a job during the day doing clothes alterations for an expensive department store. At night, she took courses in quilt-making and needlepoint, two things she had always enjoyed. When she had saved up enough money, she rented a corner of a well-established beauty parlor and opened up her own needlecraft boutique. In between helping customers, she made early American quilts which she sold to linen shops and private customers. Betty slowly built up her own circle of friends. She started to date. She also looked up relatives whom she had ignored. For the first time in her life, she had a sense of being someone and belonging somewhere.

One day, she wrote her children telling them where she lived, that she hoped they, their father, and Judy were well. She also told them that she would like to see them. Shortly after that letter, her ex-husband came to visit her in her shop. He confided in her that he had

had a lot of trouble with the children after she had left, and he had had to go into family therapy with the children. The therapist suggested that the children be permitted to see their mother.

And so, even though the children stayed with Judy and their father, they did visit their mother often and went away on vacation with her. Betty also suggested that the children go to Alateen. The therapist seconded that suggestion.

It was Betty's oldest child who said at an Alateen meeting: "I never knew what a wonderful, valuable mother I had until we admitted to ourselves, 'Yes, we have an alcoholic in the family, and her alcoholism has affected us, too!' Now we say, a recovered alcoholic is a super person—and her family and friends become super, too!"

Such statements are not unique.

Countless Bettys succeed.

For more information, visit us at www.thedrinkingwomanrevisited.com and www.answersforteens.com.

NOTES AND READINGS

Chapter 1 A WOMAN AN ALCOHOLIC—NEVER!
"Alcoholics Anonymous, a Community Resource for Coping with a National Health Problem." New York: Alcoholics Anonymous World Services, Inc., 1975. A paper.
Block, Marvin A. Alcoholism: It's Facets and Phases. New York: John Day Co., 1965. Chapter 13.
Bowman, Karl. M. and E. Morton Jellinek. "Alcohol Addiction and It's Treatment." Quarterly Journal of Alcohol Studies, 2:98–176, 1941.
Brecher, E. M. et al, eds. Licit and Illicit Drugs. Boston: Little Brown & Co., 1972, pp. 475–481.
Fielding, H. An Enquiry into the Causes of the Late Increase of Robbers, etc., with some Proposals for Remedying this Growing Evil. London: A. Millar, 1751.
Fleming, Alice. Alcohol: The Delightful Poison, A History. New York: Delacorte Press, 1975.
Foster, E. The Principles and Practices of Midwifery. London: R. Baldwin, 1781.
Horn, John L. and Kenneth W. Wanberg. "Females Are Different: Some Differences in Diagnosing Problems of Alcohol Use in Women."

University of Denver and Fort Logan Health Center, Washington, D.C., June, 1971. A pamphlet.

Keller, Mark and Mairi, McCormick. A Dictionary of Words About Alcohol. New Brunswick: Publication Division, Rutgers Center of Alcohol Studies, 1968.

Keller, Mark, "Discussion of Alcoholism in Women." Reprinted from the proceedings of the First Annual Alcoholism Conference of the NIAAA, 1973.

Schuckit, M. "The Alcoholic Woman, a Literature Review." Psychiatric Medicine, 3:37–43, 1972.

Taylor, Robert Lewis. Vessel of Wrath: The Life and Times of Carrie Nation. New York: The New American Library, 1960.

"To the Mother and Father of an Alcoholic." Al-Anon Family Group Headquarters: P.O. Box 182, Madison Square Station, New York, N.Y. 10010. A pamphlet.

Wall, J. H. "A Study of Alcoholism in Women." American Journal of Psychiatry, 93:951–952, 1937.

Warner, Rebecca H. and Henry L. Rosett, M.D. "The Effects of Drinking on Offspring, An Historical Survey of the American and British Literature." Journal of Studies on Alcohol, 36: 11, 1975.

Updates

Vaillant, George E. The Natural History Of Alcoholism Revisited. Cambridge, Mass: Harvard University Press, 1995. eBook Collection

The American Psychiatric Publishing Textbook of Substance Abuse Treatment 4th edition edited by Marc Galanter, M.D., Herbert D. Kleber, M.D. Washington D.C.; London, England 2008

Brady KT, Randall CL: Gender differences in substance use disorders. Psychiatr Clin North Am 22: 241–252; 1999

Brady KT, Grice DE, Dustan L, et al: Gender differences and substance abuse disorders. Am J Psychiatry 150:1707–1711, 1993.

Substance Abuse and Mental Health Services Administration: Facilities offering special programs or groups for women: The DASIS Report, Issue 35, 2006a. Available at: http://www.oas.sahmhsa.gov/2k6/womenTx/womenTX.htm.

Substance Abuse and Mental Health Services Administration: National Survey on Drug Use and Health. Rockville, MD, Substance Abuse and Mental Health Services Administration, 2006b. Available at: http://www.oas.sahmhsa.gov/nsduh.htm.

Chapter 2 ALCOHOL AND ALCOHOLISM DEFINED

Alcohol and Health. U.S. Department of Health, Education and Welfare, Washington, D.C., 1974. Chapter 5.

Bell, C. H., J. N. Davidson, and H. Scarborough, Textbook of Physiology and Biochemistry. Baltimore, Md.: William and Wilkins, 1968.

Curran, F. J. "Personality Studies in Alcoholic Women." Journal of Nervous and Mental Disease, 86:645–667, 1937.

Fleming, Alice. Alcohol: The Delightful Poison, A History. New York: Delacorte Press, 1975.

Garrett, Gerald R. and Howard M. Bahr. "Women on Skid Row." Quarterly Journal of Studies on Alcohol, 34:1228–1243, 1973.

Hornik, Edith L. You and Your Alcoholic Parent. New York: Association Press, 1974.

Jones, Ben Morgan, and Marilyn K. Jones. "Women and Alcohol: Intoxication, Metabolism and the Menstrual Cycle" in, M. Greenblatt, Alcoholism Problems in Women and Children. New York: Grune and Stratton, 1976.

—. "Male and Female Intoxication Levels for Three Alcohol Doses, or, Do Women Really Get Higher Than Men?" Alcohol Technical Reports. Center for Alcohol and Drug Related Studies, University of Oklahoma Health Sciences Center, Vol. 5, No.1, 1976

Mann, Marty. Neu: Primer on Alcoholism. New York: Holt, Rinehart and Winston, 1958.

Milgram, Gail G. What is Alcohol and Why Do People Drink? New Brunswick: Publications Division, Center of Alcohol Studies, Rutgers University, 1975.

Updates

Brady KT, Randall CL: Gender differences in substance use disorders. Psychiatr Clin North Am 22: 241–252; 1999

Brady KT, Grice DE, Dustan L, et al: Gender differences n substance abuse disorders. Am J Psychiatry 150:1707–1711, 1993

Ewing, John A. "Detecting Alcoholism: The CAGE Questionnaire" JAMA 252: 1905–1907, 1984

Fuchs CS, Stampfer MJ, Colditz GA, et al: Alcohol consumption and mortality among women. N. Engl J Med 332:1245–1250, 1995

Gilman SE, Abraham HD: A longitudal study of the order of onset of alcohol dependence and major depression. Drug Alcohol Depend 63:277–286, 2001

Hernandez-Avila CA, Rounsaville BJ, Kranzler HR: Opiod-, cannabis-, and alcohol-dependent women show more rapid progression to substance abuse treatment. Drug Alcohol Depend 74:256–272, 2004

Hommer D, Momenan R, Rawlings R, et al: Decreased corpus callosum size among alcoholic women. Arch Neurol 53:359–363, 1996.

Kessler RC, McGonagle KA Zhao E, et al: Lifetime and 12-month prevalence of DAM-III-R psychiatric disorders in the United States: results from the National Comorbidity Survey. Arch Gen psychiatry 51:8–19, 1994

Mann K, Ackermann K, Croissant B, et al: Neuroimaging of gender differences in alcohol dependence: are women more vulnerable? Alcohol Clin Exp Res 29:896–901, 2005

Piazza NJ, Vrbka JL, Yeager RD: Telescoping of alcoholism in women alcoholics.

Int.J Addict 24:19–28, 1989.

Randall CL, Roberts JS, Del Boca FK, et al: Telescoping of landmark events associated with drinking: a gender comparison. J Stud Alcohol 60:252–260, 1999

Sinha R, Roundaville BJ: Sex differences in depressed substance abusers. J Clin Psychiatry 63:616–627, 2002.

Nishizawa S, Benkelfat C, Young S.N, Leyton M, Mzengeza S, de Montigny C: Differences between males and females in rates of serotonin synthesis in human brain. *Proceedings of the National Academy of Sciences USA* (PNAS) vol. 94 no. 10 May 13, 1997 http://www.pnas.org/content/94/10/5308.long#abstract-1

McGill University. "Alcoholism could be linked to a hyper-active brain dopamine system." ScienceDaily. ScienceDaily, 2 August 2013. <www.sciencedaily.com/releases/2013/08/130802131843.htm>.

NOTES AND READINGS

Amit Etkin, M.Phil, Ph.D.; Christopher Pittenger, M.D., Ph.D.; H. Jonathan Polan, M.D.; Eric R. Kandel, M.D.: Toward a Neurobiology of Psychotherapy: Basic Science and Clinical Applications. The Journal of Neuropsychiatry and Clinical Neurosciences 2005;17:145–158.doi:10.1176/appi.neuropsych.17.2.145 http://neuro.psychiatryonline.org/article.aspx?articleid=101952.

UNDERAGE DRINKING Why Do Adolescents Drink, What Are the Risks, and How Can Underage Drinking Be Prevented? NIAAA Number 67, 2006. http://pubs.niaaa.nih.gov/publications/AA67/AA67.htm.

Chapter 3 YOU'RE JUST LIKE YOUR PARENTS—MAYBE?

Emerson, Haven, et al. Alcohol and Man. New York: The Macmillan Company, 1932.

Goodwin, Donald W. Is Alcoholism Hereditary? New York: Oxford University Press, 1976.

—, Fini Schulsinger, Leif Hermansen, Samuel B. Guze, and George Winokur. "Alcohol Problems in Adoptees Raised Apart from Alcoholic Biological Parents." Archives of General Psychiatry, 28:238–245, February, 1973.

Greenberg, L. A. "Is Alcoholism Inherited?" Quarterly Journal of Studies on Alcohol, 19:346, 1958.

Schuckit, Marc A., Donald A. Goodwin, and George Winokur. "A Study of Alcoholism in Half-Siblings." American Journal of Psychiatry, 128:1132–1126, March, 1972.

Seixas, F. A., GilbertS. Omenn, E. David Burk, and Suzie Eggleston. "Nature-Nurture in Alcoholism." Annals of the New York Academy of Sciences, 197:1–229, 1972.

Updates

Gelernter, J. & Kranzler Henry R. "Genetics of Addiction." The American Psychiatric Publishing Textbook of Substance Abuse Treatment 4th edition edited by Marc Galanter, M.D. Herbert D. Kleber, M.D. Washington D.C.; London, England 2008, pages 17–27.

Goodwin, DW. "Alcoholism and Heredity." Archives of General Psychiatry 36:57–61, 1979–Am Med Assoc http://pubs.niaaa.nih.gov/publications/.htm.

Prescott, Carol A. "Sex differences in the Genetic Risk for Alcoholism." Alcohol Research& Health (The Journal of the National Institute on Alcohol Abuse and Alcoholism) 26-4/264-273, 2002.

Edenberg Howard J. "The Genetics of Alcohol Metabolism." Alcohol Research& Health (The Journal of the National Institute on Alcohol Abuse and Alcoholism) 30-1/5-13, 2007.

Chapter 4 PREGNANCY

Bezzola, D. A. "Statistical Investigation Into the Role of Alcohol in the Origin of Innate Imbecility." Quarterly Journal of Inebriety, 23: 346-354, 1901.

Bible, Old Testament, Judges 13:3-4.

Jones, K. L. and D. W. Smith. "Recognition of the Fetal Alcohol Syndrome in Early Infancy." Lancet, 2:999-1001, 1973.

Jones, K. L., D. W. Smith, A. P. Streissguth, and N. C. Myrinathopoulos. "Outcome in Offspring of Chronic Alcoholic Women." Lancet, 1:1076-1078, 1974.

Jones, K. L., D. W. Smith., C. N. Ulleland, and A. P. Streissguth. "Pattern of Malformation in Offspring of Chronic Alcoholic Mothers." Lancet, 1:1267-1271, 1973.

Little, Ruth K, F. A.Schultz, and W. Mandell. "Drinking During Pregnancy." Journal of Studies on Alcohol, 37:375, 1976.

Seixas, Frank A. "Alcohol and Its Drug Interactions." Annals of Internal Medicine, 83;86-92, 1975.

Smith, D. W., K. L. Jones, and J. W. Hanson. "Perspectives on the Cause and Frequency of the Fetal Alcohol Syndrome." Annals of the New York Academy of Science. In press.

Warner, R. H. and H. L. Rosett. "The Effects of Drinking on Offspring." Journal of Studies on Alcohol, 36:11, 1975.

UPDATES

Anderson A, Hure A, Forder P, Powers J, Kay-Lambkin F, Loxton D. Predictors of antenatal alcohol use among Australian women: a prospective cohort study.

Belenko S., Peugh J.: Estimating drug treatment needs among state prison inmates. Drug Alcohol Depend 77:269-281, 2005.

BJOG 2013; DOI: 10.1111/1471-0528.12356.

Caprara DL, Nash K, Greenbaum R, et al: Novel approaches to the diagnosis of fetal alcohol spectrum disorder. Neurosci Biobehav Rev 31: 254–260, 2007.

Cohen LS, Altshuler LL, NonacsR, et al: Relapse of major depression during pregnancy in women who maintain or discontinue antidepressant treatment. JAMA 295:499–507, 2006.

Fitzimons HE, Tuten M, Vaidya, et al: Mood disorders affect drug treatment success of drug-dependent pregnant women. J Subst Abuse Treat 32: 19–25, 2007.

Mack Avram H., Barros Monica: "Forensic Addiction Psychiatry." The American Psychiatric Publishing Textbook of Substance Abuse Treatment 4th edition edited by Marc Galanter, M.D. Herbert D. Kleber, M.D. Washington D.C.; London, England 2008, pages 689–700.

Mancinelli R, Benetti R, Ceccanti M: Woman, alcohol and environment. Emerging risks for health. Neurosci Biobehav Rev 31:246–253, 2007.

Wurst FM, Wiesback GA, Metzger JW, et al: On sensitivity, specificity, and the influence of various parameters on ethyl glucuronide levels in urine: results from the WHO/ISBRA study. Alcohol Clin Exp Res 28: 1220–1228, 2004.

Chapter 5 STRESS AND FAMILY LIVING

Curlee, J. "A Comparison of Male and Female Patients at an Alcoholism Treatment Center." Journal of Psychology, 74:239–247, 1970.

—. "Alcoholic Women: Some Considerations for Further Research." Bulletin of the Menninger Clinic, 31:154–163, 1967.

"Women Alcoholics." Federal Probation, 32, No.1: 16–20, 1968.

Curran, F. "Personality Studies in Alcoholic Women." Journal of Nervous and Mental Disease, 86:645–667, 1937.

DeLint, J. E. "Alcoholism, Birth Rank and Parental Deprivation." American Journal of Psychiatry, 120:1062–1065, 1964.

Driscoll, G. Z. and H. L. Barr. "Comparative Study of Drug Dependent and Alcoholic Women." Selected Papers, 23rd Annual Meeting.

Alcohol and Drug Problems Association of North America, 9–20, 1972.

Fillmore, Kay, M. F. "Abstinence, Drinking and Problem Drinking Among Adolescents as Related to Apparent Parental Drinking Practices." A Thesis. Rutgers Center of Alcohol Studies. New Brunswick, N.J., 1970.

Freese, Arthur S. Understanding Stress. Public Affairs Committee, Inc. August, 1976. A pamphlet.

Garzon, Sally. "Alcoholism and Women." Reprinted from Alcohol Health and Research World, Dept. of Health, Education and Welfare, National Institute of Mental Health, National Clearinghouse for Alcohol Information. Washington, D.C.: 1974.

Griffiths, Edward, Celia Hensman, and Julian Peto. "A Comparison of Female and Male Motivation for Drinking." The International Journal of the Addictions, 8, No.4: 577–587, 1973. Notes and Readings 179.

Johnson, M. W. "Physicians Views on Alcoholism with Special References to Alcoholism in Women." Nebraska State Medical Journal, 50: 378–384, 1965.

Jones, M. C. "Personality Antecedents and Correlates of Drinking Patterns in Women." Journal of Consulting and Clinical Psychology, 36: 61–69, 1971.

Lindbeck, V. L. "The Woman Alcoholic: a Review of the Literature." International Journal of Addiction, 7:567–580, 1972.

Lisansky, E. S. "Alcoholism in Women: Social and Psychological Concomitants." 1. Social History data. Quarterly Journal of Studies on Alcohol, 18:588–623, 1957.

Lolli, G. "Alcoholism in Women," Connecticut Review of Alcoholism, 5:9–11, 1953.

Rathod, N. H. "Female Alcoholics," Journal of Alcoholism, 5, No.2: 60–61, 1970.

Rathod, N. H. and I. G. Thomson. "Women Alcoholics; a Clinical Study," Quarterly Journal of Studies on Alcohol, 32:45–52, 1971.

Schuckit, Marc. A. "Depression and Alcoholism in Women," Proceedings of the First Annual Alcoholism Conference. NIAAA, pp. 355–363, 1973.

NOTES AND READINGS

Selare, A. B. "The Female Alcoholic: A Clinical Study." British Journal of Addictions, 65:99.107, 1970.

Selye, Hans. Stress Without Distress. Philadelphia and New York: J. B. Lippincott Company, 1974.

Smart, R. G. "The Relationship Between Birth Order and Alcoholism Among Women," Ontario Psychological Association Quarterly, 16: 9–13, 1963.

Winokur, G. and P. Clayton. "Family History Studies. II. Sex Differences and Alcoholism in Primary Affective Illness." British Journal of Psychiatry, 113:973–979, 1967.

Winokur, G., T. Reich, J. Rimmer, and F. N. Pitts, Jr. "Alcoholism. III. Diagnosis and Familial Psychiatric Illness in 259 Alcoholic Probands." Archives of General Psychiatry, 23:104–111, 1970.

Updates

Vaillant, George E. The Natural History Of Alcoholism Revisited. Part I, Chapter 2, "The Etiology of Alcoholicsm." Cambridge, Mass: Harvard University Press, 1995. eBook Collection page 48.

Greenfield, Shelly F., Hennessy, Grace: Chapter 5, "Assessment of the Patient." The American Psychiatric Publishing Textbook of Substance Abuse Treatment 4th edition edited by Marc Galanter, M.D. Herbert D. Kleber, M.D. Washington D.C.; London, England 2008, page 59.

Greenfield SF, O'Leary G.:Sex differences in substance use disorders, in Psychiatric Illness in Women: Emerging Treatments and Research. Edited by Lewis-Hall F, William T, Panetta J, et al. Washington, DC, American Psychiatric Publishing, 20002, pp. 467–533.

Kranzler HR, Burleson JA, Brown J, et al: Fluoxetine treatment seems to reduce the beneficial effects of cognitive-behavioral therapy in type B alcoholics. Alcohol Clin Exp Res 20:1534–1541, 1996.

Pettinati HM, Volpicelli JR, Kranzler HR, et al: Sertraline treatment for alcohol dependence: interactive effects of medication and alcoholic subtype. Alcohol Clin Exp Res 24:1041–1049, 2000.

Maddux JF, Desmond DP:Careers of Opioid Users. New York, Praeger, 1981.

Green BL, Lindy JD, GraceMD, et al: Chronic posttraumatic stress disorder and diagnostic morbidity in a disaster sample. J Nerv Ment Dis 180:760-766, 1992.

Kessler RC, Nelson CB, McGonagle KA, et al: The epidemiology of co-occurring addictive and mental disorders: implications for prevention and service utilization. Am J Orthopsychiatry 66:17-31, 1996.

Conrod PJ, Pihl RO, Stewart SH, et al: Validation of a system of classifying female substance abusers on the basis of personality and motivational risk factors for substance abuse. Psychol Addict Behav 14:242-256, 2000.

Chapter 6 THE ALCOHOLIC WOMAN IN THE UNHEALTHY MARRIAGE

"Al-Anon: Living with an Alcoholic," Al-Anon Family Group Headquarters, New York City, Revised, 1960.

Fox, R. "The Alcoholic Spouse." from Neurotic Interaction in Marriage. Eisenstein, V. W. ed. New York: Basic Books, 1956.

Glatt, M. M. "A Treatment Centre for Alcoholics in a Public Mental Hospital-It's Establishment and Workings." British Journal of Addiction, 52:55-92, 1955.

Kinsey, B. A. The Female Alcoholic, a Social Psychological Study. Springfield, Ill.: Charles C. Thomas, 1966.

—. "Psychological Factors in Alcoholic Women froma.State Hospital Sample." American Journal of Psychiatry. 124: 1463-1466, 1968.

Lisansky, E. S. "Alcoholism in Women-Social and Psychological Concomitants." Quarterly Journal of Studies on Alcohol, 18:588-623, 1957.

Mann, Marty. New Primer on Alcoholism. New York: Holt, Rinehart and Winston, 1958.

Selare, A. B. "The Female Alcoholic." British Journal of Addiction, 65:99-107, 1970.

Wilsnack, S. C. "The Needs of the Female Drinker: Dependency, Power or What?" Proceeds of the Second Alcoholism Conference, NIAAA, 65-83, 1973.

Wood, H. P. and E. L. Duffy. "Psychological Factors in Alcoholic Women." American Journal of Psychiatry, 123:341-345, 1966.

Updates

Winters J, Fals-Stewart W, O'Farrell TJ, et al: Behavioral couples therapy for female substance-abusing patients: effects on substance use and relationship adjustment. J consult Clin Psychol 70:344–355, 2002.

Fuller RK, Branchey L, Brightwell DR, et al: Disulfiram treatment of alcoholism. A Veterans Administration cooperative study. JAMA 256:1449–1445, 1986.

Olmsted, M. E., Crowell, J. A. and Waters, E. (2003), Assortative Mating Among Adult Children of Alcoholics and Alcoholics. Family Relations, 52: 64–71. doi: 10.1111/j.1741-3729.2003.00064.x

Friedman H.S., Martin L.R, The Longevity Project. New York City, Hudson Street Press, March, 2011.

Chapter 7 FEMALE SEXUALITY AND ALCOHOLISM

Brecher, E. M., et al, eds. Licit and Illicit Drugs. Boston: Little, Brown, 1972. pp. 475–481.

Cramer, M. J. and E. Blacker. "Early and Late Problem Drinkers Among Female Prisoners." Journal of Health and Human Behavior, 4:282–290, 1963.

Driscoll, G. Z. and H. L. Barr. "Comparative Study of Drug Dependent and Alcoholic Women." Selected Papers, 23rd Annual Meeting, Alcoholic and Drug Problems Association of North America. pp. 9–20, 1972.

Franck, K. and E. Rosen. "A Projective Test of Masculinity-Femininity." Journal of Consulting Psychology, 13:247–256, 1949.

Garret, Gerald and Brigham Young. "Disaffiliation Among Urban Women." Quarterly Journal of Studies of Alcohol, 34: 1228–1243, 1973.

Karpman, B. The Alcoholic Woman. Washington, D.C.: Linacre Press, 1948.

Kinsey, B. A. The Female Alcoholic; a Social Psychological Study. Springfield, IL, Thomas, 1966.

—. "Psychological Factors in Alcoholic Women from a State Hospital Sample." American Journal of Psychiatry, 124:1463–1466, 1968.

Larison, Lucienne. From Woman to Woman. New York: Alfred A. Knopf, 1975.

Levine, J. "The Sexual Adjustment of Alcoholics; a Clinical Study of a Selected Sample." Quarterly Journal of Studies on Alcohol, 16: 675–680, 1955.

Lindbeck, V. L. "The Woman Alcoholic; a Review of the Literature." International Journal of Addiction, 7:567–580, 1972.

Lisansky, E. S. "Alcoholism in Women; Social and Psychological Concomitants." I. Social history data. Quarterly Journal of Studies on Alcohol, 18:588–623, 1957.

"Our Bodies Ourselves: A Book By and For Women". By the Boston Women's Health Book Collective. New York: Simon and Schuster, 1971.

Rathod, N. H.and 1. G. Thomson. "Women Alcoholics; a Clinical Study." Quarterly Journal of Studies of Alcohol, 32:45–52, 1971.

Senseman, L. A. "The Housewife's Secret Illness; How to Recognize the Female Alcoholic." Rhode Island Medical Journal, 49:40–42, 1966.

Wilsnack, Sharon C. "Sex Role Identity in Female Alcoholism." Journal of Abnormal Psychology, 82:253–261, 1973.

—. "The Effects of Social Drinking on Women's Fantasy." Journal of Personality, 42, No.1, March, 1974.

—. "The Needs of the Female Drinker: Dependency, Power or What?" Clinical Psychology Service, Massachusetts Mental Health Center, Harvard Medical School, Boston. Date unknown.

Winokur, G. and P. J. Clayton. "Family History Studies. IV. Comparison of Male and Female Alcoholics." Quarterly Journal of Studies on Alcohol, 29:885–891, 1968.

Wood, H. P. and ,E. it. Duffy.' "Psychological Factors in Alcoholic Women." American Journal of PsychiCltry, 123:341–345, 1966.

Updates

Lewis, R.W., Fugi-Meyer, K.S., Bosch R, Fugi-Meyer A.R., Laumann E.O., Lizza E. et al.: Epidemiology/risk factors of sexual dysfunction. Journal of Sexual Medicine, 1 (1), 35–39, 2004.

Wilson G.T. & Lawson D.M.: The effects of alcohol on sexual arousal in women. Journal of Abnormal Psychology 85(5), 489–497, 1976.

Schacht R.L., George W.H., Heiman J.R., Davie K.C., Norris J., Stoner

S.A. et al.: Effects of alcohol intoxication and instructional set on women's sexual arousal vary based on sexual abuse history. Archives of Sexual Behavior, 36 (5), 655–665, 2007.

Gavaler J.S., Rizzo L., Van Thiel D.H., Brezza E., Deal S.R.: Sexuality of postmenopausal women: Effects of duration of alcohol abstinence. Alcoholism: Clinical and Experimental Research 18(2), 29–271, 1994.

Sobczak, JA: Alcohol use and sexual function in women: a literature review. Journal of Addictions Nursing, 20:71–85, 2009 page 71.

Magee M, Miller D: Lesbian Lives: Psychoanalytical Narratives Old and New. Hillsdale, N.J. Analytic Press, 1997.

Cabaj P.C.: Chapter 44, "Gay Men and Lesbians." The American Psychiatric Publishing Textbook of Substance Abuse Treatment 4th edition edited by Marc Galanter, M.D. Herbert D. Kleber, M.D. Washington D.C.; London, England 2008.

Chapter 8 FEMINISM

Blane, H. T., M. J. Hill, and E. Brown. "Alienation, Self-esteem and Attitudes Toward Drinking in High School Youngsters." Quarterly Journal of Studies on Alcohol, 29:350–354, 1968.

Bowen, Murray. "Alcoholism and the Family System." Center for Family Learning, 10 Hanford Ave., New Rochelle, N. Y. 10805, Vol. I, No.1, November 1973.

Cox, D. F. and R. A. Bauer. "Self-confidence and Persuasibility in Women." Public Opinion Quarterly, 28:453–466, 1964.

Cramer, M. J. and E. Blacker. "Social Class and Drinking Experience of Female Drunkenness Offenders." Journal of Health and Human Behavior, 7:276–283, 1966.

Curlee, Joan. "Alcoholism and the Empty Nest." Bulletin of the Menninger Clinic, 33:165–171, 1969.

—. "Alcoholic Women: Some Consideration for Further Research." Bulletin of the Menninger Clinic, 31:154–163, 1967.

Doyle, Nancy. "Woman's Changing Place: a Look at Sexism." Public Affairs Pamphlet No. 509, New York, 1974.

Filmore, Kaye M. "Relationship Between Specific Drinking Problems in Early Adulthood and Middle Age." An Exploratory 20 year follow-up study. Journal of Studies on Alcohol, 36:882–907, July

1975. Rutgers University Center of Alcohol Studies, New Brunswick, NJ.

Frazer, Judy. "The Female Alcoholic." Addiction Research Foundation of Ontario, 33 Russell Street, Toronto, Ontario M5S2sl, 1974.

Gomberg, Edith S. "Alcoholism and Women: State of the Knowledge Today." Paper presented at the National Alcoholism Forum in Milwaukee, Wisconsin, April 29, 1975.

Hanson, D. J. "Drinking Attitudes and Behavior Among College Students." Journal of Alcohol and Drug Education, 19:6-14, 1974.

Helson, R. "The Changing Image of the Career Woman." Journal of Social Issues, 28:33-46, 1972.

Horn, John L. and Kenneth W. Wanburg. "Females are Different: Some Difficulties in Diagnosing Problems of Alcohol Use in Women." University of Denver and Fort Logan Mental Health Center, Washington D.C., June 25-26, 1971.

Johnson, M. W. "Physician's Views of Alcoholism with Special Reference to Alcoholism in Women." Nebraska State Medical Journal, 50:378-384, 1965.

Jones, R W. and A. R. Helrich. "Treatment of Alcoholism by Physicians in Private Practice, a National Survey." Quarterly Journal of Studies on Alcohol, 33:117-131, 1972.

Knupfer, G. "Female Drinking Patterns." 15th Annual Meeting of the North American Association of Alcoholism Programs, 1964. Selected papers, 140-160.

Lisansky, Edith. "The Woman Alcoholic." The Annals of the Academy of Political and Social Sciences, 351:73-82, 1958.

Norris, J. L. "A.A.'s Membership Survey." Paper read at the North American Congress on Alcohol and Drug Problems, San Francisco, December 18, 1974.

Parker, F. B. "Sex Role Adjustment in Women Alcoholics." Quarterly Journal of Studies on Alcohol, 33:647-657, 1972.

Saltman, Julie. "The New Alcoholics: Teenagers." Public Affairs Committee, Inc. New York, 1973. A booklet.

Siassi, I., G. Crocetti, and H. R. Spiro. "Drinking Patterns and Alcoholism in a Blue-Collar Population." Quarterly Journal of Studies on Alcohol, 34:917-926, 1973.

Sterne, Muriel W. and David J. Pittman. "Drinking Patterns in the Ghetto." Social Science Institute, Washington University, St. Louis, 1972.

Straus, R. and S. D. Bacon. Drinking in College. New Haven: Yale University Press, 1953. p. 72.

Tamerin, J. S., C. P. Newman, and M. H. Marshall. "The Upper-Class Alcoholic: a Syndrome in Itself?" Psychosomatics, 12:200–204, 1971.

"To the Mother and Father of an Alcoholic." Al-Anon Family Group Headquarters, P.O. Box 182, Madison Square Station, New York, N.Y. 10010.

Trotter, T. "An Essay, Medical, Philosophical and Chemical on Drunkenness and its Effects on the Human Body." Boston: Bradford and Reed, 1813.

Wechsler, Henry, and Mary McFadden. "Sex Difference in Adolescent Alcohol and Drug Use. A Disappearing Phenomenon." Quarterly Journal of Studies on Alcohol, 37: 1291–1301, 1976.

Wilsnack, Sharon C. "The Effects of Social Drinking on Women's Fantasy." Journal of Personality, 42, No. 1:43–61, 1974.

—. "The Needs of the Female Drinker: Dependency, Power or What?" Clinical Psychology Service, Massachusetts Health Center, Harvard Medical School, Boston. Date unknown.

—. "Sex Role Identity in Female Alcoholism." Journal of Abnormal Psychology, 32:253–261, 1973.

"Women and Alcoholism in Industry." Paper read by W. L. Wallace, Annual Conference on Women and Alcoholism, Our House, at the YWCA, Detroit. June 19, 1974. Mimeographed.

Updates

Journal of Occupational and Environmental Medicine. "Alcohol use disorders linked to decreased 'work trajectory.'" ScienceDaily. ScienceDaily, 1 July 2014. <www.sciencedaily.com/releases/2014/07/140701101326.htm>.

Schwartz C R,.Han H: The Reversal of the Gender Gap in Education and Trends in Marital Dissolution, American Sociological Review V 79 (4): 605–629, 2014

Employed Female Admissions to Substance Abuse Treatment, SAMHSA's Newsletter Volume 18, Number 4, July/August 2010 http://www.samhsa.gov/samhsanewsletter/Volume_18_Number_4/WorkingWomen.aspx.
Friedman H.S., Martin L.R, *The Longevity Project*. New York City, Hudson Street Press, March, 2011. pages 146–147.

Chapter 9 THE CULTURAL STRESS FACTOR: I

Alcohol Abuse and Black America-Frederick D. Harper, ed. Alexandria, Va: Douglass, 1976.
Baum, Charlott, Paul Hyman, and Sonya Michel. The Jewish Woman in America. New York: Dial Press, 1976. pp. 3, 7, 8.
Davis, Fred T., Jr. Alcoholism: Needs of Minorities. National Council on Alcoholism, New York.
Garrett, Gerald, Brigham Young. "Disaffiliation Among Urban Women." Quarterly Journal oi Studies on Alcohol, 34: 1228–1243, 1973.
Garrett, G. R. and H. M. Bahr. "Women on Skid Row." Quarterly Journal of Studies on Alcohol, 34:1228–1243, 1973.
Klein, Isaac, translator, The Code ot Maimonides. Book Four: The Book of Women. New Haven and London: Yale University Press, Yale Judaica Series, pp. 133–134.
Larkins, John R. Alcohol and the Negro: Explosive Issues. Zebulon, No. Carolina: Record Publishing Company, 1965.
Malzberg, Benjamin. Studies of Mental Disease Among Jews. Albany, New York: Research Foundation for Mental Hygiene, Inc., 1971.
Milman, Doris H., and Wen-Huey Sue. "Patterns of Drug Usage Among University Students: V. Heavy Use of Marijuana and Alcohol by Undergraduates." Journal ot the College Health Association, 21:181–7, 1973.
Pettigrew, Thomas F. A Profile of the Negro in America. New York: D. Van Nostrand, 1964. pp. 53–54.
Schmidt, W., and Popham, R.E., "Impressions of Jewish Alcoholics (Ontario)." Quarterly Journal of Studies on Alcohol, 37:931–939, 1976.
Scott, G. Blacks in the Liquor Industry. New York: Black Enterprise, 1975. pp. 6, 33–37 and 48.

Sterne, Muriel W. and David J. Pittman, Drinking Patterns in the Ghetto. Social Science Institute, Washington University, St. Louis, 1972.

Updates
Oslin DW: Late-life alcoholism: issue relevant to the geriatric psychiatrist. Am J Geriatr psychiatry 12:571–583, 2004.
SAMHSA: Substance abuse among older adults: treatment improvement protocol #26. Rockville, MD, U.S. Department of Health and Human Services, 1998.
Herd, D. The influence of religious affiliation on sociocultural predictors of drinking among black and white Americans. *Substance Use & Misuse* 31:35–63, 1996.
Taylor, R. J.; Mattis, J.; and Chatters, L. M. Subjective religiosity among African Americans: A synthesis of findings from five national samples. *Journal of Black Psychology* 25:524–543, 1999. http://pubs.niaaa.nih.gov/publications/arh26-4/251-256.htm.
Pearson WS, Dube SR, Nelson DE, Caetano R. Differences in patterns of alcohol consumption among Hispanics in the United States, by survey language preference, Behavioral Risk Factor Surveillance System, 2005. Prev Chronic Dis 009;6(2):A53.http://www.cdc.gov/pcd/issues/2009/apr/08_0039.htm.

Chapter 10 THE CULTURAL STRESS FACTOR: II
De Beauvoir, Simon. The Coming of Age. Translated by Patrick O'Brien. New York: Warner Paperback Library, 1973.
Kuttner, Robert E. and A. B. Lorincz. "Promiscuity and Prostitution in Urbanized Indian Communities." Mental Hygiene, 54:79–91, 1970.
Levy, J. C. and S. J. Kunitz. Indian Drinking: Navajo Practices and Anglo-American Theories. New York: Wiley, 1974. p. 19.
May, S. N. The Crowning Years. Philadelphia, 1968.
Molinari, Carol. "Alcoholism: Alaska's Number 1 Health Problem." Alcohol Health and Research Warld. Experimental Issue, Summer, 1976. pp. 3–4.
Moss, Bertram B. Caring for the Aged. Garden City, N. Y.: Doubleday, 1966.

NOTES AND READINGS

"Older Problem Drinkers." Alcohol Health and Research World. Experimental Issue, Spring, 1975.

Rosin, Arnold J. and M. Glatt. "Alcohol Excess in the Elderly." Quarterly Journal of Studies on Alcohol, 32:53–59, 1971.

"Self-Help Programs for Indians and Native Alaskans." Alcohol Health and Research World. Experimental Issue, Summer, 1974.

Zimberg, Sheldon. "The Elderly Alcoholic." Gerontologist, 14:221–224, 1974.

Updates

Keoke, Emory Dean, and Kay Marie Porterfield. "Aztec public drunkenness laws." Encyclopedia of American Indian Contributions to the World: 15,000 Years of Inventions and Innovations. New York: Facts On File, Inc., 2001. American Indian History Online. Facts On File, Inc. http://www.fofweb.com/activelink2.asp?.

Anwalt P. R., Berdan FF: The Codex Mendoza. Sci Am 266:70–79, 1992.

Lucey M. R., Hill E.M., Young J.P, Demo-Dananberg L, Beresford T.P, "The Influences of Age and Gender on Blood Ethanol Concentrations in Healthy Humans." Journal of Studies on Alcohol and Drugs, Volume 60, 1999 > Issue 1: January 1999.

Beauvais F., American Indians and Alcohol: Spotlight on special populations, pubs.niaaa.nih.gov Vol. 22, No. 4, pages 253–259, 1998. http://pubs.niaaa.nih.gov/publications/arh22-4/253.pdf.

Beauvais F.,ED. Indian adolescent drug and alcohol use: Recent patterns and consequences <Special Issue>. American Indian and Alaska Native Mental Health Research 5 (1):1–78, 1992.

Hisnanick J.The prevalence of alcohol abuse among American Indians and Alaska Natives. Health Values 16 (5): 32–37, 1992.

Jilek W., Native renaissance: The survival and revival of indigenous therapeutic ceremonials among North American Indians. Transcultural Psychiatric Research Review 15: 117–147, 1978.

Mail P. D., and McDonald D.R., Tulapai to Tokay: A Bibliography of Alcohol Use and Abuse Among Native Americans of North America. New Haven, CT: HRAF Press, 1980.

May, P.A.Alcohol policy consideration for Indian reservations and bordertown communities. American Indian and Alaska Native Mental Health Research 4 (3): 5–59, 1992.

Chapter 11 LIFE WITH AN ALCOHOLIC

Ackerman, Nathan W. *Treating the Troubled Family.* New York and London: Basic Books, Inc., 1966.

Boche, Leonard. *Continuum of Care.* Association of Halfway House Alcoholism Programs of North America, Inc., 1969.

Bowen, Murray. *Alcoholism and the Family System.* Center for FamilyLearning, No.1, November 1973.

Curlee, Joan. "Alcoholism and the Empty Nest." *Bulletin of the Menninger Clinic,* 33: 165–171, 1969.

"Dilemma of the Alcoholic Marriage, The." Al-Anon Family Group Headquarters, Inc., New York, 1971.

Fox, Ruth. "The Alcoholic Spouse in Neurotic Interaction." In *Marriage,* Eisensteen, V. W., ed. New York: Basic Books, 1956.

—. "The Effects of Alcoholism on Children." From the proceeding of the V International Congress on Psychotherapy. *Progress in Child Psychiatry.* pp. 55–56 Basel/New York: Karger, 1963, reprinted by NCA in pamphlet form.

Jackson, Joan K. and Kate L. Kogan. "Search for Solutions: Help Seeking Patterns of Families of Active and Inactive Alcoholics." *Quarterly Journal of Studies on Alcohol,* 24:449–472, 1963.

"'What's Next? Asks the Husband of the Alcoholic.'" Al-Anon Family Group Headquarters, Inc., New York, 1966.

Updates

Hornik-Beer E. L., *For Teenagers Living With A Parent Who Abuses Alcohol/Drugs.* An Authors Guild BackInPrint.com Edition, iUniverse LLC Bloomington, Indiana, 2013.

Chapter 12 ALCOHOLICS ANONYMOUS

Alcoholics Anonymous. New York: AA Publishing, Inc., 1955.

Alcoholics Anonymous, A Community Resource For Coping With a National Health Problem. New York: Alcoholics Anonymous World Services, Inc., 1975.

Alcoholics Anonymous Comes of Age, by a co-founder. New York: Harper & Bros., 1957.

"AA's 1974 Membership Survey." Paper by Dr. John L. Norris, North American Congress on Alcohol and Drug Problems, San Francisco, December 18, 1974.

How AA Members Cooperate with Other Community Effort to Help Alcoholics. New York: Alcoholics Anonymous World Services, Inc., 1974.

Updates

Friedman H. S., Martin L.R, *The Longevity Project*. New York City, Hudson Street Press, March, 2011 pages 155–156.

Chapter 13 SEEKING HELP

Ackerman, Nathan W. Treating the Troubled Family. New York: Basic Books, 1966.

Bissell, LeClair and A. J. Mooney. "The Alcoholic Physician." Resident and Staff Physician, 22:55–59, 1976.

Blane, Howard T. *The Personality of the Alcoholic Guises of Dependency*. New York: Harper & Row, 1968.

Browne-Mayers, A. N., E. E. Seelye, and L. Sillman. "Psychosocial Study of Hospitalized Middle-Class Alcoholic Women." Annals of the New York Academy of Science, 273:593–603, 1976.

Coleman, James H., and Wm. E. Evans, "Drug Interactions With Alcohol." Resident and Staff Physician, 22:3441, 1976.

Fox, Ruth, "The Alcoholic Spouse in Neurotic Interaction," In Marriage, Eistensteen, V. W., ed., New York: Basic Books, 1956.

—. "The Effects of Alcoholism on Children" from the Proceedings of the V International Congress on Psychotherapy, Progressive Child Psychiatry, Karger, Basel/New York: 1963. Reprinted by NCA in pamphlet form.

Goldwater, Eugene. "Practical Ways to Help Patients Who Drink Too Much." Resident and Staff Physician, 22:22–26, 1976.

Jackson, Joan K. and Kate L. Kogan. "The Search for Solutions: Help Seeking Patterns of Families of Active and Inactive Alcoholics." Quarterly Journal of Studies on Alcohol. 24:449–472, 1963.

NOTES AND READINGS

Kinsey, Barry A. *The Female Alcoholic, a Social Psychological Study.* Springfield, Ill.: Charles C. Thomas, 1966.

Rudolph, Margaret. "The Addicted Woman in the Community." Association of Halfway House Alcoholism Programs of No. America, Inc., St. Paul, Minn., 1975.

Vincent, Terry. "When to Use Dilantin During Withdrawal." Resident and Staff Physician, 22:50–51, 1976.

Wall, James H. "A Study of Alcoholism in Women." American Journal of Psychiatry, 93:943–952, 1937.

Updates

Prochaska, J. O., DiClemente C. C., Norcross, J. C.: In search of how people change: applications to addictive behaviors. Am Psychol. 9:1102–1114, 1992.

Hornik-Beer E. L., *For Teenagers Living With A Parent Who Abuses Alcohol/Drugs.* An Authors Guild BackInPrint.com Edition, iUniverse LLC Bloomington, Indiana, 2013.

McLellan A. T., Kushner H., Metzger D. S., et al: The fifth edition of the Addiction Severity Index. JSubst Abuse Treat 9:199–213, 1992.

The American Psychiatric Publishing Textbook of Substance Abuse Treatment. 4th edition edited by Marc Galanter, M.D., Herbert D. Kleber, M.D. Washington D.C.; London, England 2008

Simpson, DD: A conceptual framework for drug treatment process and outcomes. J Subst Abuse Treat 27:99–121, 2004.

McLellan, AT, Chapter 7 in *The American Psychiatric Publishing Textbook of Substance Abuse Treatment* 4th edition edited by Marc Galanter, M.D., Herbert D. Kleber, M.D. Washington D.C.; London, England 2008, page 103.

Friedman H. S., Martin L. R., *The Longevity Project.* New York City, Hudson Street Press, March, 2011.

Chapter 14 GETTING READY TO FACE THE WORLD AGAIN

Beecher, Marguerite and Willard. The Mark of Cain: An Anatomy of Jealousy. New York: Harper and Row, 1971.

Bergman, Rita E., ed. *Children's Behavior*. New York: Exposition Press, 1968.
Berne, Eric. *Games People Play*. New York: Ballantine Books, 1973.
Freud, Sigmund, *Collected Papers*, Volume 4. Authorized translation under the supervision of Joan Riviere. New York: Basic Books, 1954.
Reik, Theodor, *Myth and Guilt, The Crime and Punishment of Mankind*. New York: George Braziller, 1957.

www.ingramcontent.com/pod-product-compliance
Lightning Source LLC
LaVergne TN
LVHW011153080426
835508LV00007B/375